VOICES FROM THE VEIL

OF

SILENCE:

BEREAVEMENT

AND

LIFE AFTER DEATH

BY GEORGE A. HOVER

TO MARK

January 16, 1963 – August 26, 1981

*JOGGING IN THE
DARK*

ACKNOWLEDGEMENTS

More than many, this book has been written only with help from a large number of intellectual and spiritual kindred spirits.

There is evidence that in the background, always, Mark Hover has kept on pushing for me to deal with the issues of life, death, and life after death, and to write this book. After Mark, huge thanks go to my wife Carol, always supportive, and a good intellectual critic and endless reader of manuscripts. Heartfelt thanks also go to my children, and children-in law, all six highly educated in the sciences: Karen Hover, Francois Amar, Franz Hover, Susie Carter, Anne Severns and Mark Severns. All have offered encouragement, criticism, and clear scientific thinking to correct my occasional sloppiness.

Other friends, mostly manuscript readers, have been extremely helpful and encouraging, especially Diane Potter, Dean Chapman, Tom Taylor, Carla Johnston, Carol Johnson, Charles Churchill, Janet and Dean Preston, Bill Peek, Bob Reber, Jean Bragan, Richard Lang, Trudy Duffy, Rick and Suzanne Myers.

Also, thanks to the many people through the years who have shared their stories with me, and who have helped organize and have attended workshops and classes I have produced on these topics, especially Margaret Herbert, Herbert Hover, Terry Pontius, Susan Lowery, Pam and Jerry Sine, Pam Pinault, Terry Powell, Beth Folsom, Donna Burk, Beverly Blaisdell, Greg and Marianne Black, Mounir Elkatib, and Judy Lang.

Much computer and technical support have come from Judy Lee Trautman who took me from being non-owner of a computer to relative proficiency.

My sister, Janet Hover Preston, has been a fellow traveler on this journey, and kindly created the moving illustrations.

Special thanks go to Judith Price Justus, of Perrysburg, Ohio, an author, musician, and fellow believer, who has labored with all the details of editing and has been exceptionally encouraging.

Finally, as I have tried to argue in Chapters One and Two, there is evidence that in the background, always, Mark Hover has kept on pushing for me to deal with the issue of life, death, and life after death, and to write this book.

PREFACE

This book has been over 22 years in the writing! It is the unlikely product of events set in motion by the death of my oldest son, Mark, in 1981 in a tragic accident. My family and I grieved – painfully, and we've memorized the normal stages of grief by going through them. Almost all the literature on grief suggests that when this process is done, people "move on" and that life once again becomes "normal."

But in our case, some other very strange events were happening. For example, my children and other people were telling me of riveting paranormal events in which it looked as though Mark was still communicating. Through workshops and counseling, I met hundreds of other people who had lost loved ones, and who told the same kinds of stories. I needed to become acquainted with some of the important researchers who have studied the question of life after death. A handful of psychics, some of whom appeared to be in touch with Mark, assaulted my skepticism. Recently, I have been teaching workshops on Life After Death Studies and writing curriculum materials for the United Methodist Church.

In this book I have tried to put down information that may be of help to bereaved people. If I had discovered this material earlier myself, the grief process might have been much less painful. I simply did not know of the thousands of case reports that suggest life exists after the death of the body. Even more important, I had no idea that many skeptical materialistic people, including scientists, have changed their minds about this very issue after reading some of the research material.

But the implications of survival research also go far beyond offering comfort to bereaved people, important as that is.

We learn that tragedy and bereavement, when combined with a certainty about life after death, can have a robust and positive impact on religious faith, regardless of our religious tradition.

Growth in spirituality can put us in touch with new people, and other religious traditions, so that our lives become richer.

Our lives grow deeper and calmer as we learn about mysticism and non-ordinary states of consciousness. These have a long history, and exploring them can help offset the pervasive materialism of our own culture.

In a culture where many people describe life as a treadmill, and seem not to have much sense of meaning in their lives, exploring these "deeper" dimensions of life can help us discover our own life's meaning.

There are serious intellectual reasons for pursuing this study as well. For scientific intellectuals, a new thrust in the disciplines of psychology, religion, anthropology, and sociology has been developing in the last several decades. Ernest Becker and others suggest that much human evil and suffering rise out of deeply buried "death anxiety." If this is true, the discovery of the strong evidence for life after the death of the body offers serious therapy for "death anxiety." A scientific underpinning for confidence in life after death can make huge positive changes in human behavior. Moreover, physicists like David Bohm, (1917-1991) Erwin Schrodinger, (1887-1961) and others remind us that there may be connections between modern physics and the so-called psychic phenomena.

For literary intellectuals, it may not be well known that paranormal events, especially the components of the Near Death Experience have been described in classical prose, poetry, drama, the visual arts and cinema. A partial list of authors would include Willa Cather, Ernest Hemingway, Peter Carey, Mark Littleton, Edgar Allen Poe, Ambrose Bierce, Katherine Porter, Jonathan Swift, Edna St. Vincent Millay, Thornton Wilder, C.S. Lewis, Plato, Homer, Virgil, Dante. (For a fuller listing, see "The Significance of the Near Death Experience In Western Cultural Traditions" by Alan Pew at alanp46@msn.com). Moreover, apparitions have been explored by Washington Irving, William Shakespeare (sometimes called "Scary Shakespeare"), Henrik Ibsen, and A.C. Doyle. Robert Frost, Jack London, Johann Goethe, E.P. Oppenheimer, and A.C. Doyle have entertained reincarnationist themes in their work, and there are extensive sacred texts in Hinduism, Sikhism, Jainism, and Buddhism dealing with reincarnation. Out-of Body Experiences have been mentioned or described by Aristotle, St. Augustine, Plato, Leo Tolstoy, Walter De la Mare, August Strindberg, Guy de Maupassant, Ernest Hemingway, Carl Jung, and William Gerhardi. There is of course an explosion of popular literature, TV and film treating these subjects.

Education, especially moral education, for many of us used to involve the promise of heaven and the threat of hell. These ideas no longer seem valid for most well-read or "enlightened" people. But the "life review" in Near Death Experiences, and the profound emotional changes that happen to people who have these and other experiences can provide a new basis for moral education. John C. Gibbs at Ohio State University has done research on the NDE as a tool in moral education. Life after Death Studies is already being used in other religious education settings.

For all of these reasons, this journey has been painful, life changing, and energizing, and my book is an effort simply to pass it on.

TABLE OF CONTENTS

PROLOGUE

"The stairs gradually ascend to a place no one knows of. Many stood, wondering, compelled to begin the lengthy climb, but are restrained by the bitter world of reality.

He puts his foot on the first step, trying desperately to break loose. A force like that of a high-voltage magnet grew more intense, trying to break his grip on the golden rails.

The quiet whistle of an unobstructed electro-cardiogram was all he could hear. The doctors rushed to get his heart to beat once more, but to no avail. When they tried to stimulate with voltage, the magnets' forces pulsated, but gradually weakened.

"God damn it. I cut too deep! I cut too deep!" he heard the helpless doctor cry, but now it was over with.

> He was free.
> No more bone breaking hits.
> No more hurting,
> No more of the brutal, violent world of college
>   football.
> He was free!

Sure, they'd miss him. Sure a few may cry. Sure, he was another tragic victim of the dangers of stick-tackling. But they would all join him when they were ready.

It was the ecstasy of his life. Naked girls pranced and danced all around him, touching him, kissing him. They gradually undressed him from his battle field outfit, throwing the pads and cloth to the bottom where he would never have to see it again. Lukewarm water showered down, washing him of the mud and sweat.

The warm soft fur of whining kittens and puppies brushed softly against his ankles. They all had syringe holes on them somewhere, where the Humane Society had injected the life-ending serum.

A soft whisper, like that of wind gushing through pine trees became more intense as he made his way up the staircase. The animals followed him: The Pied Piper. "Oh, my God! No! Oh God! a voice trilled from the base of the staircase. He turned. "Mom?"

Written by Mark Allen Hover, age 18, a few weeks before his death in a pedestrian/truck accident.

CHAPTER ONE

WHAT A STORY!

"Because it is sometimes so unbelievable, the
truth escapes becoming known."

Heraclitus (c. 500 B.C.)

The author lives near the Maumee River, a large muddy river, with agricultural runoff. Muddiness seems to be part of nature. This book presents over 170 cases touching on life after death of the physical body. The muddy plus the clearer cases have to be taken together. They both affect human emotion and hence the impact of personal awareness.

Some stories are true, but nearly too strange to be believed. This one begins on August 26, 1981, a hot summer's day in the northwest corner of Ohio. Early in the morning, I was working in the basement with my youngest son, David. Basement floor-painting is not my favorite task, but I always enjoyed David's company and we work well together. Suddenly there was a loud, insistent knock on the front door. A uniformed police officer asked if I were George Hover, and asked permission to enter. He spoke – the most gut-wrenching, heart-rending words a parent can hear: "I'm sorry to have to tell you this. Your son Mark Hover was killed in an accident this morning in Athens, Ohio." I was nauseated and faint, and leaned over the stairs to catch myself from retching or passing out. The officer said that Mark had been hit by a large truck while he was jogging, and was killed instantly. It happened on an expressway near Ohio University, two hundred miles south of Toledo, Ohio where we lived in a nearby suburb. He had been in Athens only a week, and was jogging early in the morning to get in shape for the football season. My head knew that it was true, but my heart wouldn't believe it.

We were in shock, and the shock shielded us from pain, but only for the first few hours. Family and friends arrived, and so did Mark's girlfriend, Denise. I vaguely remember playing ping pong in the backyard - anything to detract from the nausea that had returned by then, along with the pounding heart, and the pressure in my head. I even remember that thoughts of suicide crossed my mind for a moment when I had a knife in my hand picking rhubarb. For a Methodist minister, this was unthinkable. Knowing the state of my despair, my wife Carol came out to check on me.

But the worst pain was thinking of the pain Mark must have felt, the excruciating slap of pain. It was a huge semi, loaded with tires, and apparently his torso went under the truck. The visibility was poor, and the driver said, according to the police report, that he thought he hit a deer, pulled over to look, and found to his horror that he had run over and crushed a young man.

We did not blame the driver. There was very thick fog that morning. Some months later, a letter came from his wife, saying that he had suffered a near nervous breakdown over the event, and that he had changed his career because of it. We wondered, did Mark even know what had happened? We could hardly bear to think about it, but Mark went through it! We hoped that any sensation and feeling of body pain was short. But what of his dreams and hopes for an exciting football career, for becoming a meteorologist, or a writer, or a conservation professional, and a father and a lover? And how could that strong body, that intensity, that affection for his family and friends – how could that be snuffed out in seconds? Is life really that fragile? For years, I have thought about what might have gone through his mind after the impact but before physical death. And for several years, every semi-truck I saw triggered the memory of what had happened to Mark.

Mark was born on January 16, 1963, a snowy night in Boston. I was a student at that time, and Mark's mother, Diane, was a nurse. His was a breach birth, but he was not a large baby, so we thought he would not have any problems. Mark seemed more fussy than some children, but healthy, strong and inquisitive. As his brother and sisters came along, he was loving and protective, if sometimes temperamental with them. Always an avid athlete, he did well in school in spite of a problem with reading that was corrected when he was in junior high school.

When his mother and I separated in early 1973, Mark was ten, and he was the most visibly upset of all our four children. His anger and depression came out mostly in his temper, and in a fierce competitiveness in table games like cards, monopoly and scrabble. He was especially intense when he competed in athletics. After my divorce, Carol came into our family in 1974, and related beautifully to Mark as she did to all the children. Mark got along well with friends, and loved fishing, football, and music, like any healthy teenager. He especially loved his dog, Elfie. As he entered high school, we began to see that he was a gifted athlete, and built for football. At the end of his senior year, he weighed about two hundred and thirty pounds, was six feet four inches tall, and had won a scholarship to play football at Ohio University. Playing defensive tackle in a large university football program requires strong determination, and Mark certainly had that. (Later in this chapter I will describe his determination to communicate with his family after his death.) But with all that athletic ability, Mark also had a side that was intelligent, reflective, and gentle, and expressed itself in his creative writing and his love of music. He must have played "Stairway to Heaven" at least a thousand times on the piano, and after his death we discovered in his papers a short story about a young man, killed on the football field, who has a near death experience, climbs a stairway and enters into the light. Looking back, we think that matters of life and death preoccupied him more than we knew, and we remember that he had a dream in the spring before he was killed that frightened him badly. Now we think he knew something of his coming death.

There is one very funny story that shows the relationship Mark had with Carol and me. We had used time-out as a way of discipline for years. Normally it involved a ten minute stay in the bathroom. One day, Mark and David were kicking each other under the table. I was tired, and said, "Time Out! Mark, go to the downstairs bathroom, and David upstairs." Mark, aged eighteen, with his two hundred and thirty pounds of football muscle, stood up, all six feet four inches of him, and said, "I like the bathroom," and he went into the downstairs bathroom! And David went upstairs!

Like most people in our culture, I had not really thought much about death, even though I was trained as a United Methodist minister, had graduated from a theological seminary, and served churches as a pastor for twelve years. My mother had died six years before, but one expects sickness and death with older people, and most do not ask quite so many questions when a parent dies. But an eighteen year old with his whole life before him? It was an unspeakable loss, to the world of course, but mostly to Mark. He had come to love life, had great success, was looked up to by many, and could become anything he wanted to become. And of course we wondered, would we ever see Mark again? Does love somehow bridge the gap between life and death? There was a huge hole in our lives, and even in the lives of our extended family and close friends.

The shock and the flurry of activity in planning a memorial kept the pain away for several days. But when it descended it was like a smothering black cloud and it lingered in the back of my mind for many, many months. Friends and family could not have been more supportive, but grief is an all-encompassing and lonely business.

Two days later the memorial was held in his hometown of Maumee, Ohio, with an overflow crowd, including the entire football team from Ohio University. Classmates reported how much they admired Mark, and one football player even said that he wished he could hold Mark's hand again! A week later, when Ohio University football team played the University of Toledo at Toledo in football, they announced that they had lost a valuable player with a bright future, and honored Mark at halftime. After that, we had only pictures of Mark, his ashes, a souvenir football from a high school championship game, a collection of his poems and short stories, and our memories. When I went back to work as a family therapist, some clients were so kind that they insisted that I talk about my loss before they would talk about the problems that brought them to therapy. Life somehow lumbered on.

I went through the normal stages of grief as outlined by Elizabeth Kubler-Ross: denial and isolation, anger, bargaining, depression, and acceptance. Each person goes through these stages at his/her own pace, and sometimes not in the order in which they are listed. Mine began with denial, and I recall only believing that Mark's death was real when we saw the body after our local mortician brought it back from Athens. Then came the anger. I remember lying and pounding on the floor, as tears fell to the carpet. Probably I was more than irritable during that time, but no one commented about it. Fortunately I did not use alcohol, drugs or indulge in obsessive work to avoid the pain. I think I just felt it vibrating in every cell of my body. This went on for months, especially at times when I was alone. I thought no one, except Carol, and probably other bereaved parents, could understand what it is like to lose a child. Tears, questions, more tears, more questions, and long conversations moved us slowly but naturally through the normal grieving process. For me the bargaining took something of an unusual form. I wanted desperately to have things as they were before, which meant in some way seeing Mark again. I did not bargain with God, but thought, perhaps if I can learn to become more spiritual, or even trigger my own out-of-body experience, I could then see Mark on another level of reality. (I have become far more spiritual, and even felt several times that I had triggered an OBE, but never felt that I encountered Mark in that context.)

The final stage of acceptance came much later, and I identify one event in particular, though some might say this is evidence of denial. In a Michigan restaurant, eating alone, I suddenly had the realization, after all my study on the project, that the evidence for life after death is very strong. I was astonished, and it was such an emotional realization that I wanted to stand on a table and announce to everyone that death is not the end and that my son is **not dead, but alive**. I restrained myself. I knew that my grief stricken life would never be the same again, and from that day, things improved rapidly. Fortunately my marriage and family have held together in spite of everything, with a renewed appreciation and gratitude for one another, and for everything Mark was to each of us.

On the day of Mark's death, I remember calling the American Society for Psychical Research in New York, and asked for the Director of Research, Dr. Karlis Osis. He suggested two books. One was Kenneth Ring's book, *Life At Death,* on near death experiences. The other was Osis' own new book, *At the Hour of Death,* on deathbed visions. After that call, I called a family I had worked with as a family therapist, and told them to cherish their children, because I had lost one of mine.

I was by no means confident about life after death, even though I was a minister and had the presence of mind to call the American Society for Psychical Research for help. I had also not been impressed by the various movies that purported to touch on the issue of life after death: "The Exorcist," "Poltergeist," "The Amityville Horror," and the later ones, "Ghost," "The Sixth Sense," "Dragonfly," and others. I thought they trivialized the whole issue of grief and survival after death. I was more interested in serious research.

But within days after his memorial service there began an astonishing series of after-death communications from Mark, and they have continued for over twenty years, to the present. Initially I thought they were products of my imagination, or the imaginations of family members and psychics. I had been trained to be skeptical, especially by my study of psychology (the science of the soul). All people are at times victims of wishful thinking and I suspected that belief in life after death was one of those products of human kind's wishful thinking and fear of death. It was also a matter of pride: I certainly did not want to be a fool, or to have people think that grief had clouded my judgment! I had especially mixed feelings about working with psychics. I desperately wanted evidence that Mark was somehow all right, but I knew that a few psychics prey on the vulnerability of grief stricken people. It is not hard to manipulate the thinking of desperate people. But after years of study and working with psychics, I learned that there are many talented and genuine psychics, including nearly all of those I worked with. Only people who are ignorant of the serious research with psychics dare to dismiss the research and the psychics out-of-hand. And this is true of the other strands of research on the question of life after death.

As I've said, in the Michigan restaurant I had experienced that sudden and emotional awareness that the evidence for life after death is very strong. But gradually, in spite of my skepticism, I was also understanding that not only was the evidence strong, but that the communications from Mark were also strong. These communications were coming from different directions, through different people. And I was very happy to hear from Mark, and happy that there were not just one or two communications, but many, and they kept happening, through many years. This may seem to readers to be the most unbelievable part of the story.

THOUSANDS OF SIMILAR REPORTS

After years of study and a good number of communications from Mark, almost all of my skepticism is gone. Why? There are thousands of cases reported of events that are very like the things that happened in our family and in my work with psychics.[1] The existence of similar reports does not prove life after death, of course, but does lend a measure of legitimacy, and suggests that this material is important, and not only to the writer. When nearly identical after death communications happen independently to many people, this is a form of the repeatability that is so important in scientific research. In these cases the repeated events are not in the lab, but in life. I think the important lesson for me to learn was that a healthy skepticism includes being skeptical of that very skepticism! Now, I think that Mark was trying to communicate to his family that he is alive and active on some other level of existence. And in recent years, the communications, independently, through a number of different psychics, have been that Mark very much wants me to write this record. In this book, I hope to show why I believe this is true.

So in the next chapter is a straightforward report of the uncanny events that have convinced me of Mark's survival of death. Some of the events are very impressive, others are open to some questions. After each story of events that happened in our family, I give an example of a nearly identical report by someone else whose uncanny experience caused them to believe that they also were being contacted by a deceased loved one. In the case of Mark apparently making a prediction about a future war, I have added a report by Carl Jung of his vision of the coming of World War I. Jung's vision, however, was not transmitted through a psychic.

FOOTNOTE

1. Readers who would like to verify that there are indeed thousands of cases, many carefully investigated, are referred to the well- known researchers of the 20th century, and authors of the more contemporary popular works. Most of these are listed in the Bibliography at the end of the book. They include, among many others, Edmund Gurney, Frederick W.H. Myers, William Barrett, Carl Becker, C.J. Ducasse, Camille Flammarion, Hornell Hart, Raynor Johnson, Herbert Greenhouse, Alan Gauld, Raymond Bayless, D. Scott Rogo, Karlis Osis, Kenneth Ring, Nils Jacobsen, Michael Sabom, Ian Currie, Robert Almeder, Melvin Morse, Bill and Judy Guggenheim, Carla Wills-Brandon, Gary Schwartz.

CHAPTER TWO

EVIDENTIAL ANECDOTES

"The same stream of life that runs
through the world runs through
my veins night and day and dances
in rhythmic measure. It is the same
life that shoots in joy through the dust
of the earth into numberless blades
of grass and breaks into tumultuous
waves of flowers."

Rabindranath Tagore
Nobel Prize, 1913

FEELING A TOUCH

It was two days after Mark was killed, and early in the morning. We had not had much real sleep because of the shock of his death, and I think that I was neither awake nor asleep. Everything was very still, both in the house and outside. Suddenly I felt a heavy arm around one shoulder and across my chest. It was mostly a physical sensation, rather than the sensing of a presence. I simply thought Carol had turned over and thrown an arm over me, but when I looked, she was asleep and lying on her side, facing the opposite direction. The sensation was so pronounced that I may have cut it short after twenty seconds or so, by assuming someone else was in the room. Astonished, I looked around but no one was there that I could see. Then I remembered that Mark had died, and only then the thought crossed my mind, "This is too good to be true. I must be hallucinating since I want so badly to see Mark again." My skepticism was very much alive.

A similar report: A former army sergeant lost a fourteen year old son in Florida. "After my son's funeral, we started to leave the cemetery. My mother was driving the car, and my wife was sitting alongside of her. I was sitting alone in the back seat. I felt Keith's presence at my left side. He put his arm over my shoulder and kept it there as we rode all the way back to our house. I could feel his body pressing up against me, and I could feel his warmth beside me. I detected that everything was all right. I got a peaceful, quiet, comforting feeling. This lasted about twenty minutes, until we got to the driveway, and then Keith was gone. I have no doubt whatsoever. I'm absolutely sure that this happened."[1]

HEARING A VOICE

Several evenings later, at bedtime, I was lying in bed, exhausted with all that had happened, and almost asleep. I thought I heard a voice: "Hey Pop, I'm home." I went downstairs to see if anyone was there, and found no one. Only after walking down the stairs did I remember that this was Mark's typical announcement when he arrived home late in the evening, after a football game or a date. I remember saying to myself, "Either Mark is here or I am losing my mind!"

A similar report: "...Mrs. Gladys Watson...was awakened from a deep sleep by someone quietly but insistently calling her name. As she roused and sat up, she was astonished to see her paternal grandfather, to whom she was devoted, leaning toward her. He looked perfectly real and lifelike. There was a pleasant smile on his face. "Don't be frightened," he reassured her in a warm, affectionate voice. "It's only me. I've just died." Mrs. Watson woke her husband, who reminded her that her grandfather was fine, and alive. But because she was so upset, he made a phone call and found that indeed his wife's grandfather had died a few minutes earlier.[2]

THE CAT REACTS

Mark had a close and stable relationship with his high school girlfriend, Denise. A year younger than Mark, Denise was a lovely young woman, dark-haired, pretty, happy, and bouncy. We were grateful that Denise was in Mark's life, and she was open and always friendly with our family, even maintaining contact for years after she joined the military and married. We had regular contact with Denise through those painful days after Mark's death. One day she told us that more than once, her cat, Wong, who used to sit on Mark's lap, behaved as though there was someone or something in her room. He would wander around, looking in different directions, but Denise never found anything to explain the cat's behavior, so she assumed that Mark was somehow visiting her. She did not seem to doubt it, and thought Mark's presence with her and her cat was the most natural thing in the world. Mark had been friendly with Denise's whole family, and had spent many hours at their home.

A similar report from Sweden: "Father, mother, brother, and I in the kitchen. Kille lay in his basket, he was the world's worst watchdog: he loved people, good and bad alike, and never barked. 'Someone's coming,' said my brother, listening to sounds from the gravel path. We all heard steps – they rounded the corner of the house and approached the kitchen door. Kille started growling deep down in his stomach. Someone knocked on the door. ... Kille raised a thick ruff around his neck – the hair stood straight up. Mother walked over to open the inner door; then Kille rose up cautiously, his body stiff as a board and his hair on end. Just as she was opening the outer door, Kille flew like lightning out of his box, barking loudly, and rushed into the wood-storage room and disappeared under the stove there. Outside there was *nothing*. ... Father and my brother went outside with candles to see if a tramp was there, but found nothing. The next day one of mother's relatives came and told us that one of our close relatives had died. Later when I reminded mother of what happened, she only answered curtly, 'Yes, that was the evening Mans Nilsson died.'" [3]

SOMETHING ABOUT A TREE

Several intuitive friends were kind enough to spend time with me following Mark's death, even though they knew that I was quite skeptical about psychic work. Some people wish to distinguish between mediums and psychics. Psychics, I am told, see things happen and report what they are seeing or feeling. Mediums will appear to become the voice of the deceased, or sometimes say that during trance, the spirit of the deceased temporarily takes over their mind and body. Early, classic research with mediums dealt with events of this sort.

I have worked with both mediums and psychics, in Ohio and Maine, and these talented people have been supportive, helpful, and remain good friends after many years.

One intuitive friend, J.J., has also been an important part of this story from the beginning. We met in one of those uncanny connections through a series of events that involved a concert, and another person. I was speaking with this person during the concert and told her about my interest and asked if she knew any intuitive people who might help me to understand the paranormal things that were happening. She said a lady had just given a talk to her Association for Research and Enlightenment group, but she had to ask permission first before giving me her name. J.J. agreed, so I called her and then began a series of fascinating meetings. One evening J.J. was meeting with me and two other people, D.A. and D.B. On that particular evening we were working with an alphabet board, and Mark communicated with them. Mark spelled out the message, "Denise and I put a quarter under a split-trunk tree near the tombstone of ___ in Riverside Cemetery. It is dated 1976."

This cemetery is less than a mile from our home, and overlooks the Maumee River. The cemetery, not large as cemeteries go, is old, and had been severely damaged a few years before by a huge flood and ice flow that broke down the iron fence and smashed many of the tombstones. I recognized that this could be a serious test of the authenticity of the message as well as Mark's ability to communicate. If only we could find the tombstone, and the tree, and the quarter, and if Denise could confirm that in fact she and Mark had deposited it there.

Something About a Tree

The next morning, Good Friday, was a cold, blustery day. The sky was as gray as the river, and there were fast moving white clouds, like the rapids when the river is low. In the cemetery, with no hills and few trees, the wind itself sounded like the howling from a haunted house. Perhaps the first Good Friday was like that too. There were four of us searching – three ladies and myself, but the tombstone with the name on it was nowhere to be found. We must have walked and searched for nearly an hour, and were cold and disappointed. We were about to give up, but J.J. finally found a tombstone with a name that sounded remotely like the one we were looking for, and near it was a yew tree with a double trunk, as Mark had said. Under the tree, J.J. used her keys to dig up the soil, and there was a dirty quarter, with the date of 1976! I wanted desperately to believe that indeed Mark and Denise had hidden the quarter, but my skepticism had not left me. This would be too good to be true, would it not? I didn't know D.B., and I wondered if perhaps she had planted the quarter. I was not nearby when J.J. found the quarter, but she wiped off the dirt, and remembers that dirt stuck in the round part of the 6. By the time I joined J.J., the quarter had been cleaned, and I remember thinking, "A quarter buried that long would not be clean." Only later did I learn that it was not pristine, but that J.J. had wiped off the dirt.

The only way really to confirm the paranormal aspect of the event would be to ask Denise. Now, 22 years later, Denise confirms that indeed she and Mark used to walk to Riverside Cemetery, and "There was something about a tree," but she is not able to confirm anything about a coin. Was this a hoax? Was it a fragmented communication from Mark? None of the women knew Mark, yet even if one of them had planted the coin, part of what she said was true, and apart from personal acquaintance with Denise, there was no way she could have known of the walks to the cemetery and "Something about a tree." This highlights a perennial problem in work with psychics: sometimes they are uncannily right, and profoundly wrong at the same time. Also, if Denise did not remember a quarter, but something about a tree, does it suggest the quarter was "planted" or simply that Denise forgot? In this event, we simply don't know, but it underlines the universal difficulty of dealing with psychic matters.

A similar but more convincing report from North Carolina: "Mr. J.P. Chaffin, whose father had died nearly four years previously, dreams on a number of occasions that his father appears at his bedside. On the last occasion his father is wearing his old black overcoat, and shows him the pocket, saying, 'You will find my will in my overcoat pocket.' ...Mr. Chaffin searches the pocket of his coat, and finds therein a roll of paper which reveals the location of a hitherto unsuspected second will."[4] This case is famous and was investigated by the American Society for Psychical Research. The case went to probate and the inheritance was redistributed on the basis of the will found by J.P. Chaffin. Several of J.P. Chaffin's friends and family members confirmed that events had happened as Chaffin reported them.

THE YELLOW DOORS

About two weeks after Mark's death, Carol and I were eating breakfast, and David, Mark's sixteen year old brother, came into the kitchen and reported a dream. "Mark and I were eating peanut butter sandwiches in the kitchen. I knew that he was dead, so I asked him, 'How did you get out of your body?' He said, 'When I got to the yellow doors there were two of me, and I took a new body.'" After Mark's accident, I had begun reading several books on near-death experiences, and I knew that near-death experiencers sometimes report a split in which the "spirit" is outside the body watching the medical procedures. Mark was killed in Athens, Ohio, and we had not gone there but had the body brought back to Toledo by the local mortician. I knew that since Mark had been killed instantly, his body had been picked up by the mortician in the college town, rather than by an ambulance. I found out the name of the mortician, wrote a letter, and asked if his hearse or ambulance had any yellow doors. He kindly sent back a letter and photographs. The van in which the body was picked up was shown with its back doors open. They were bright yellow! In the research on apparitions, this is called a "veridical apparition" in which the apparition of the deceased gives verifiable information not previously known by the survivors.

The Yellow Doors

A similar report from the Southwest: "Cody came to me in a dream. He appeared happy and healthy. I saw him as a child, but he seemed older. He talked to me and related to me almost like he was an adult. He said there was something wrong with his tombstone – that it was on a little girl's grave who had died two weeks before he did. He told me that his name was backwards. The next day I went out to the cemetery, and there was no tombstone where Cody was buried. I called the monument company and asked them when they were going to put the stone on my son's grave. They said it had already been placed out there two weeks earlier. Then I went to the caretaker of the cemetery and asked him where the newest gravestones were. He took me to a grave, and there was Cody's tombstone. I asked the caretaker whose grave it was. He looked at the chart and said it was a little girl who had died on October 1st. Cody had died on October 14th. All the other tombstones were facing in one direction, but this one was turned around facing the other way. To Cody it must have looked like his name was backwards! Finally, the monument company came out to the cemetery and put the tombstone on Cody's grave correctly."[5]

THE RUSSIAN BOX

About two months after my son Mark's death, his next younger sister, Kathy, had a dream. She reported at breakfast one morning that she had dreamed that Mark was sitting on the bed in his parents' bedroom, surrounded by neighborhood children. He was instructing them that they should never use marijuana. At the very time Kathy was reporting the dream, David, who was now sleeping in Mark's basement bedroom, came into the kitchen. He was carrying a box, hand carved in Russia, which we had not seen since before Mark went away to college. Astonished, I asked David where he had gotten the box. He said, "I was just lying in bed and had a feeling that I should look above the tiles in the ceiling above the bed. That's where I found it." What was in the box? We opened it and found a small amount of marijuana that Mark had hidden there when he went to college. (He didn't want the illegal drug found if we moved away from the house.) Kathy did not know where the box was, and David did not know of Kathy's dream. And telepathy between Kathy and David does not seem to explain it either, since neither knew of the box. Again, I think Mark was communicating, this time by arranging events between two of his siblings. Then I found a number of similar reports; this one even involved finding something in a bedroom!

A similar report from Idaho: "When Grandpa Davis died, my mother-in-law, Grandma Davis, was left alone. Her family all lived some distance away from her. My husband's brother would visit her and go through his father's things – his guns and his hunting and fishing equipment – and take them out the back door. But somehow he missed the one gun that was Grandpa's special pride. It was an old army rifle that had a hand-carved stock. ... My husband loves guns and had a particular attraction to that one. At Grandma Davis' death everybody looked for that old gun, but nobody could find it. We were all so busy getting things out of the house that I was extremely exhausted and fell asleep for about two hours. During that time, Grandma Davis came to me. She was at the foot of the bed and looked like she always did. She told me the rifle was between the mattress and the box spring of the bed I was sleeping on. I felt she wanted my husband to have it. I woke up and called my husband to come into the room. I pulled the mattress up and showed him where the rifle was. He was so shocked and surprised, and he asked me how I knew. I said, "Grandma Davis told me where it was."[6]

TEDDY BEAR

I recognized that the story of the yellow doors and the Russian box might be of interest to those doing research on life after death. I wrote a letter to Dr. William Roll, a well known parapsychologist then teaching at Duke University, where a great deal of research on telepathy had been done from the 1950s by Dr. J.B. Rhine and others. Dr. Roll invited me to come to Durham where he was studying a Canadian medium, Mrs. K., who had flown to Durham from Ottawa for this study. Dr. Roll's interest in this study was to see what physiological changes happen in the body of the medium when she is in trance. The medium, already familiar to Dr. Roll, was wired to take GSR, EKG, EEG and other readings. I said nothing as I went in, and was not introduced. As Dr. Roll is a well known professional researcher, I assumed that he had told the psychic nothing about me or my family, or Mark's death.

The medium began to ramble, then said she thought she was talking to a young man whose name began with M. She said a number of things that made no connections for me, including, "Your son is talking about a teddy bear, not a toy, but a coach or a teacher. Did he have someone like that named Teddy?" I said I did not think so, and the session ended. I was disappointed but also thought the whole exercise was rather silly. I flew home, five hundred miles, and reported to Carol what the medium had said, including the mention of a teddy bear. Carol, David, and Anne reminded me, "Don't you remember, Mark used to call one of his football coaches Teddy Bear because he is overweight?" It was true, but I had forgotten it.

A similar report: "So then I rang a medium, a charming lady in her seventies and asked for a seance. I was so doubting that I requested to remain anonymous. I went there with a tape recorder. The old lady fell into a trance, and in that state she told me about thirty facts she couldn't have known under any circumstances, since I was anonymous and she didn't know where I came from. Finally she mentioned my wife's name and told me that she said, 'If you want to make me happy, you must go on living and making friends!' And then she told me about how she saw her standing leafing through loose sheets of paper. I knew immediately – they were my poems. Overwhelmed, I left. I realized I must continue to live, even if it would be difficult, because I wanted to make her happy. Where no religious concepts had helped, contact with a medium did help me."[7]

A WONDERFUL BIRTHDAY

A few weeks following the events at Duke University with the Canadian medium, the same medium offered to come to our home to meet with our family. I picked her up at the airport in Windsor, Ontario. Among other things, she said that Mark wanted the medium to communicate to his youngest sister, Anne, that "Something wonderful will happen on your birthday." Anne was about thirteen years old at that time, and assumed that, if the words meant anything, something would happen on her next birthday. In fact, she had a birthday party in a camper trailer and assumed that was the "something wonderful." But that was not the last of it. Sixteen years later, on her birthday, Anne's male friend, Mark, with whom she was not yet engaged, gave her a pearl necklace, saying that he had always planned to give a pearl necklace to the woman he hoped to marry. But there was still more. Exactly two years later, on her birthday, Anne and Mark were married in a beautiful wedding by the sea.

A similar report: in his book, *The Afterlife Experiments,* Gary Schwartz reports an event in one of his laboratory experiments on mediumship. The sitter was Pat, whose son had committed suicide, and the psychic was John Edward. John Edward spoke of seeing an older man along with Pat's son. They were connected, he said, and Edward assumed the older man had also died. "They're showing me...one seems to be like a husband figure to you. Do you understand that?" Pat said, "Yes," though her husband, Mike was still very much alive. "So I see this being like if the soul is the driver of a car, the car would be the body, the car was running, but the driver was not in it." Mike, in the weeks following, seemed to be concerned about his own death, and at one point told Pat that he did not expect to make their thirtieth anniversary. Pat had also had a vision of a white vehicle crashing into a tree. On the day before their thirtieth anniversary, Mike veered off the road, hit a tree, and was dead before the emergency medical team arrived.[8]

PREDICTION OF POLITICAL EVENTS?

As in the two stories above, *precognition* is perhaps the most mysterious of the paranormal events, but is well documented in research, especially by Dr. J.B. Rhine at Duke University. In 1987, while we were together in a group, J.J. said she was informed that Mark was present and was saying that an airplane would crash, and a major conflict would occur in four years. With predictions of this sort, it seems impossible to know whether the prediction really comes from the deceased, or whether it is an informed guess on the part of the medium. In any event, for most of us there was no knowledge at that time of the airplane to crash in Lockerbie, Scotland, that Saddam Hussein would invade Kuwait, which led to Desert Storm. There was also mention of a fight in a desert, about which we could know nothing, and we did not know either that tensions would break out into genocide in Bosnia in 1992, and that the United Nations would later intervene in Kosovo.

Sometime also around 1987, the ladies reported that Mark was predicting that a Bush would win the presidency "later." We knew of course that G.H.W. Bush was hoping for election in 1988, but with the knowledge of the Bush campaign at that time, "later" seemed to suggest another campaign, which G.H.W. Bush lost in 1991 but G.W. Bush won in 1999. The ladies were elated when they remembered Mark's prediction.

A similar report in which political events are predicted: Carl Jung, M.D., wrote, "Toward the autumn of 1913 the pressure which I had felt was in me seemed to be moving outward, as though it were something in the air. The atmosphere actually seemed to be darker than it had been. ... This feeling grew more and more intense. In October, while I was alone on a journey, I was suddenly seized by an overpowering vision: I saw a monstrous vision covering all the northern and low-lying lands between the North Sea and the Alps. When it came to Switzerland, I saw that the mountains grew higher and higher to protect our country. I realized that a frightful catastrophe was in progress. I saw the mighty yellow waves, the floating rubble of a civilization, and the drowning bodies of countless thousands. Then the whole sea turned to blood. This vision lasted about one hour. I was perplexed and nauseated, and ashamed of my weakness. ... That winter someone asked me what I thought were the political prospects of the world in the near future. I replied that I had no thoughts on the matter, but that I saw rivers of blood. The visions would not let me be. I asked myself whether these visions pointed to a revolution, but could not really imagine anything of the sort. And so I drew the conclusion that they had to do with me myself, and decided that I was threatened by a psychosis. The idea of war did not occur to me at all."[9] Several years later was the beginning of World War I.

TAKE SOME ACTION

During the years 1997-2002, several friends and psychics, both in Ohio and Maine, and most strongly J.J., independently reported having the impression that some young man was nearby and wanting for her to tell me to "get busy" or "get in gear." I had a sense that this involved writing about this topic. Was Mark still at work? Or did these friends and psychics themselves want me to write? But if Mark was not involved, why would this handful of people have such consistent messages and be so interested?

A similar case of communication involved writing, and involved several psychics: Frederick Myers, perhaps the greatest of the scientific researchers on life after death, wrote the huge volume, <u>Phantasms of the Living</u>, with hundreds of life after death related cases. After his own death, messages began to come to three psychics, one in India, one in Britain, one in the U.S. that, when put together, made sense. Instructions were also given to each psychic where to send her report of what she had received. These are called the "Cross-Correspondences" and, for people willing to study the material, give striking evidence of life after death. Myers, after his death, apparently wanted several people to <u>take some action.</u>[10]

HOW CAN A SKEPTICAL, EDUCATED, PROFESSIONAL PERSON TAKE ALL THIS SERIOUSLY?

Strangely enough, the study of modern scientific methods and the philosophy of science has helped me to recover from much of my skepticism. When the reader encounters through this book the names of F.S.C. Schilling, Robert Almeder, Carl Becker, Carl Jung, the reader will have met thinkers who go far beyond the superficial and fashionable skepticism of our rather materialistic culture. These writers can be met especially in Chapters 3,6,7,8. Thoughtful readers will find their skepticism under serious assault.

Here is how that happened. First, I began to recognize that there are many valid approaches to scientific research. Such research always means keen observation. But it also means clear and open minded thinking. It does not always mean repeatability in a laboratory, as in some branches of science.

Here are several examples: 1. Astronomers who study the birth and death of stars do not try to alter the behavior of the stars, or get them to repeat their birth or death. 2. Drug researchers do not expect that 100 percent of patients will respond to the same drug in the same way. 3. Few people would claim that a flipped coin cannot land on its edge, though most people have probably never seen it happen, and would not see it with repeated tries.

The German philosopher, F.C.S. Schiller makes clear something that it is easy for us to forget: "Single facts can never be 'proved' except by their coherence in a system. But, as all facts come singly, *anyone who dismisses them one by one is destroying the conditions under which a conviction of new truth could arise."* (My italics)[11]

In short, the subject we are studying influences the kind of research that can be used. In studying life-after-death research, we are often dealing with events that are rare, and described in the vocabulary of the people who experience them. So the major research forms in use are: 1. The case report, in which an event is described as accurately as possible. 2. Observation of repeated patterns, as in reports of Near-Death-Experiences, Deathbed Visions, and Out-of Body-Experience reports. 3. Laboratory experiments, as in Charles Tart's study of Miss Z., in Chapter Five. 4. Meta-analysis, described by Gene Glass as the analysis of analyses – a statistical analysis of a large collection of analysis results, for the purpose of integrating the findings.

In layman's terms, we believe that the evidence for life after the death of the physical body is very strong. Yet, because of the nature of the subject material, the kind of "proof" that is claimed in some areas of science may never be available on this issue. But a genuine search for truth does not allow us to use the convenient explanations of coincidence, fraud, hallucination, or sloppy research without a careful examination of the evidence. Meta-analysis shows that the findings of parapsychology are not due to chance, and these analyses are repeatable.

My own view, after these years, is that the many separate experiences in my family, by themselves, were suggestive. When combined with the other thousands of documented and undocumented cases, they became convincing. When I learned the various methods of research and how to measure validity in the results, I became even more convinced. And when I considered that in almost every spiritual tradition through history there has been a confidence in some form of life after death, I became more than convinced of life after death. Vast numbers of people, from various cultures, for millennia, have good reasons for their common beliefs. And in Christianity, my own tradition, the very foundation of the faith is the reports of many about seeing the risen Christ. It is not reasonable to think that all these early church reports are wrong, and that ancient and modern reports and research are all misguided. For me, such hyper-skepticism was a result of my being too confident that everything can be given a physical explanation, and that what we don't understand must be a fraud. Carl Jung considered such skepticism fashionable, but not reasonable, and refused to participate in it.

On the other hand, my skepticism has not vanished! There are several topics that could have been treated in this book but have not been. One is the so-called electronic voice phenomenon. Some researchers say that they have recorded voices through manipulation of electronic devices, especially radio, and that the voices come from the deceased. There is a certain logic to the research, since we may find that "spirits" consist of some bio-electric or bio-magnetic pattern that persists in time and space, and it is said that Thomas Edison made a box to pick up "spirit voices." But after listening to a number of purported voices, I did not find them convincing, and have not pursued the study.[12]

Another area on which I could have written is the work of Edgar Cayce, especially as it touches on the research on reincarnation. I have declined doing this for several reasons. One is that while it is fascinating, the Cayce material presents a great deal of theosophical (literally: wisdom of God) speculation, with internal consistency, but when we get to specifics, like whether his medical readings really helped specific individuals, or whether his reincarnation readings match verifiable past events, we find that the data are not verifiable due to lack of records. There are voluminous records of what Cayce said, but not of actual results in the lives of people for whom he gave readings. The Association for Research and Enlightenment, according to G. Gordon Melton, Director of the Institute for the Study of American Religion, is much less interested in what most of us would call research, but more in evangelism, organizational and educational activities.[13] This may have considerable value for people attracted to it. But as research, the study of apparent spontaneous past life memories, past life regressions in hypnosis, children's past life memories, and birthmarks and reincarnation offer a far better basis for belief, or disbelief, in reincarnation.

All this being said, there are several reasons for writing this book. One is to bring a number of investigated and sometimes older cases to modern readers. These are familiar to researchers, but not to lay persons. Another is to present a variety of cases. There are few if any recent COLLECTIONS that offer examples of the different kinds of cases. For example, Osis and Haraldsson in *At the Hour Of Death,* present cases related to deathbed visions, but not to out-of-body experiences or reincarnation. Raymond Bayless, and Alan Gauld present cases of apparitions, but not of other kinds of events. Stevenson is interested primarily in reincarnation. Sparrow presents cases of encounters with Christ. The recent book *Hello From Heaven* by Bill and Judy Guggenheim presents a wider range of reports, but these have not been investigated in the way that many of the others have been. To these I have added about twenty of my own cases. Readers can tell which are original cases since they do not have footnotes. So this collection, while not by any means complete, offers a respectably broad representation of different kinds of life after death vignettes. Here we will present cases in areas of near death experiences, deathbed visions, out-of-body experiences, apparitions, reincarnation, and after death communication. The case presentations will be followed by a brief section on analysis of the evidence for life after death. Readers interested in more detailed analysis will find good material in the works cited in the Bibliography.

There are several other purposes:

1. To comfort and encourage those who have lost loved ones. I have shown my own way of dealing with Mark's death, but others will deal with loss of a loved one in their own ways. We never truly let them go of those we love, and a certainty of their continuing life and an openness to hearing from them can make things so much easier, for our deceased loved ones and for ourselves.

2. To honor Mark, whose persistence through the years, even after the death of his body, has been a major motivator for this work.

3. To honor the many people who have helped me and my family deal with our grief and have encouraged the writing of this record.

4. To show how the findings in the research converge with the wisdom of many spiritual traditions, including those described in the New Testament record. Overall, they confirm the insights of the great world religions.

5. To give evidence from my own experience, from workshops that I have led, from case reports, from research, and from my own spiritual tradition, that the death of the body is only a transition to another level of being. Like Mark's, our life, calling, and mission continue on.

FOOTNOTES:

1. Bill and Judy Guggenheim, *Hello From Heaven*, Bantam Books, New York, 1995, page 56.
2. Ian Currie, *You Cannot Die*, Somerville House, Toronto, 1998, pages 21-22.
3. Nils Jacobson, *Life Without Death*, Dell Publishing Company, New York, 1974, Page 110.
4. Alan Gauld, *Mediumship and Survival*, William Heinemann Ltd., London, 1982, page 223.
5. Bill and Judy Guggenheim, *op.cit.*, pages 285-286.
6. Ibid., page 277.
7. Nils Jacobson, *op.cit.*, pages 132-133.
8. Gary Schwartz, *The Afterlife Experiments*, Pocket Books, New York, 2002, pages 163-171.
9. Nils Jacobson, *op.cit.*, page 62.
10. Ian Currie, *op.cit.*, pages 394-399, gives a brief overview of this complicated material.
11. Cited in Susy Smith, *The Enigma of Out of Body Travel*, Helix Press, New York, 1965, pages 121-122.
12. Interested people can contact Mark Macy, at http://www.worlditc.org, or read his recent book, *Conversations Beyond the Light*.
13. See "Edgar Cayce and Reincarnation: Past Life Readings as Religious Symbology" in *Syzygy: Journal of Alternative Religion and Culture*, Volume 3, Numbers 1-2, 1994. Also see http://www.ciis.edu/cayce/melton.html

CHAPTER THREE

NEAR DEATH EXPERIENCES

"There is only a single supreme idea an earth:
The immortality of the human soul.
All other profound ideas by which men
Live are only extensions of it."

Dostoyevsky
Diary of a Writer

Near Death Experiences have been described for centuries, and in classical literature, notably by Tolstoy in *Anna Karenina* and *The Death of Ivan Ilyitch*. From a scientific perspective, Near Death Experiences have been widely explored and discussed in the past thirty years since Raymond Moody's and Elizabeth Kubler-Ross's groundbreaking work in the 1970's. Many people believe the NDE provides strong evidence of life after the death of the body, though it is not, as many people think, the only or strongest indication of survival of death. Still, it is the most widely known of spiritual experiences suggesting another level of existence. Other evidence is given in the following chapters of this book.

People who study NDEs define the NDE as an experience reported by brain-active but comatose, or brain-inactive patients who, when they are resuscitated, tell of one or more of the markers for the NDE. There are several different listings of these markers. George Gallup, Jr. of the Gallup Poll found that about one person in twenty had an NDE, and listed the elements and their percentage of frequency as follows:[1]

Element	Percent
Out of Body	26
Accurate Visual Perception	23
Audible Sounds or Voices	17
Feelings of Peace, Painlessness	32
Light Phenomena	14

Many different researchers have given us important insights. For example, early studies showed that about 40% of people near death reported NDEs, but since that time the percentage has been shown to be smaller. There is considerable evidence that neither drugs, pychological conditions nor religious belief cause NDEs. One of the strongest and most dramatic findings is that the great majority of NDEers have significant emotional, belief, and life style changes following the NDE, and almost always are convinced that there is a life after death. Kenneth Ring discovered that even people who only *hear* about the NDE have profound and lasting life changes.

There are different kinds of NDEs, and we will divide them in this way, though nearly all are life-changing in important ways.

1. Children's NDEs
2. Unpleasant or Hell-like NDEs
3. Pleasant of Heaven-like NDEs
4. Verifiable NDEs
5. Life Changing NDEs

CHILDREN'S NDES

Children's NDEs are especially engaging. Children are thought to be more naïve, less influenced by religious or cultural expectations, and so more likely to "tell the truth." The matter-of-factness in these reports almost seems itself a proof against cleverness, or fraud. Nevertheless, children are most likely to report figures that fit with the culture where they live. There are some important exceptions to this, such as Cory in case #4 in Chapter Four.

1. I SAW TWO ANGELS

Kurt, aged seven, nearly died from muscular dystrophy compounded by pneumonia. After being without a heartbeat for three minutes, he was interviewed just hours after his resuscitation.

"I saw Bonnie, and said 'hi' to her. Then everything became dark and I saw two angels." Not one to waste time, Kurt then packed a lot of action into moments he was without heartbeat. There was a beautiful place, with flowers and rainbows, and he says that everything was white "...like it had its own light." This self-luminosity is a common feature in NDEs. He says that he talked to people, including Jesus, and that Jesus wanted him to stay. "I wanted to stay there, but we decided I had to come back and see my parents again." Finally, Kurt said that he would not be afraid to return to that place.[2]

2. I KNEW IT WAS HEAVEN

June, an eight year-old girl, nearly drowned in a swimming pool when her hair became caught in a drain. According to the report, her heart had not been beating for the forty five minutes she had received CPR.

"All I remember was my hair getting stuck in the drain and then blacking out." This sounds as though it all happened in a momentary way. Then June said the next thing she knew was that she had floated out of her body. She says she could see herself under the water, yet also that she was not afraid. "All of a sudden I started going up a tunnel, and before I could think about it, I found myself in heaven." She knew it was heaven, she says, because everything was bright and everyone was cheerful. "A nice man asked me if I wanted to stay there. I thought about staying, I really did." Then she decided that she wanted to be back with her family and "I got to come back."[3]

3. I DIDN'T KNOW IT WAS ME

A nine year old, whom Moody calls Nina, had an NDE while she was undergoing an appendectomy.

"I heard them say my heart had stopped, but I was up at the ceiling watching." She says she could see everything from up there, since she was floating close to the ceiling, but when she saw her body, said "I didn't know it was me." Then she went out into the hall and saw her mother crying. Nina asked her why, but her mother could not hear her. "Then a pretty lady came up and helped me because she knew I was scared. We went through a tunnel and went into heaven." She describes beautiful flowers, and said she met God and Jesus. They told her that she had to go back with her mother, that she had to finish her life. "So I went back…" She elaborated on the tunnel, saying it was long, and very dark, that she had gone through it "real fast." and that there was light at the end. Finally, she said "I want to go back to that light when I die…. The light was very bright."[4]

4. YOU'D BETTER GIVE UP ON THIS ONE

Robert Moss tells of an NDE that happened to him when he was nine years old. Compared to other children's matter-of-fact reports, we have the sense that his childhood experience has been elaborated by his adult verbal ability. He was rushed to a hospital in Melbourne, Australia with appendicitis, and the doctors worried that he would not survive the operation since he had hardly survived recent bouts with pneumonia. The doctors told his mother,

"You'd better give up on this one. He's never going to make it."

While on the operating table, he says, "I stepped out of my body… and flowed through the door and along the corridor…" There he saw his mother crying and his father with his arms around her. Then he "flowed" to a window and saw the brightness and the colors of spring; he says he even saw young lovers seated at a sidewalk table. He could feel the pull of the ocean, so he floated through the glass to see the beach, but instead followed a bird and soared over the city. As he entered the gate of an amusement park, suddenly he plunged into darkness. "I tried to reverse direction, but something sucked me downwards." Then, he reports, it seemed as if he tumbled down a mineshaft, for miles, and then fell into a different world. There was dimly visible what looked like a large fire pit, then "A giant with skin the color of fine white ash lifted me high above the ground, singing. The people of this world welcomed me." The people were tall, elongated, and very pale, he states, and he was required to *dream,* both alone and with others, as part of his schooling. This went on for years, in the NDE, and he became a father and grandfather, then saw his own funeral and the funeral pyre, and traveled with the smoke as his own used physical body burned. Then, "As I spiraled upward, I was entranced by the beauty of growing things…" but then he "…burst through the crust of the earth…" into a city environment, complete with cars and hot asphalt, and suddenly was "…shooting back into the tormented body of a nine year-old boy in a Melbourne hospital bed." This story has some earmarks of a shamanic journey as well as some of the typical NDE components. (A shaman is a priest or holy man who uses paranormal techniques for curing diseases, understanding hidden things, and controlling or facilitating events.)[5]

5. I TRIED NOT TO COME BACK

Caresse Crosby tells the story thirty years later as an adult of her drowning at age seven. She describes in some detail her sensations of salt water in her lungs, feeling her head expanding and exploding, like a cotton ball fluffing out. As her mind cleared, she says, "…not only did I see and hear harmony, but I understood everything." Then, like a bubble, she rose to the surface of the water, through a wooden platform, and to a place where she could see everything beneath her. She saw her father working on his boat, and her brothers, frightened, holding her feet and her hair "…like seaweed, pulled flat against the submerged bottom of the boat." Then she watched her brothers run toward home and "I saw the efforts to bring me back to life, and I tried not to come back." This reluctance to "come back" is a common theme in NDEs. And "…that moment in all my life has never been equaled for pure happiness." She wonders if perhaps she has glimpsed the freedom of eternal life. "One thing I know, that Nirvana (a Buddhist version of heaven) does exist between here and the hereafter - a space of delight, for I have been there."[6]

6. SO VERY YOUNG FOR AN NDE

Several years before Moody's book, *Life After Life* was published, this very early report came from two psychiatrists, Glen Gabbard and Stuart Twemlow. In 1972 almost no one, including children, knew about NDEs.

Todd was only two years and five months old when he bit into an electrical cord. His mother discovered the accident some two or three minutes after it happened, noticed he was not breathing, and called an ambulance. At the hospital, about twenty five minutes passed in which Todd had no heartbeat or respiration. He was unresponsive and his pupils were dilated, and he remained so for several days. It took four to six months before he regained his cortical and neurological functioning, but eventually he suffered no permanent brain damage. Here we see again the fatter-of-fact nature of reports of children.

About three months after his third birthday, his mother asked if he could tell her what he remembered when he bit the electrical cord. Todd told her, "I went in a room with a very nice man and sat with him." Asked what the room looked like, Todd said "It had a big bright light in the ceiling." Asked what the man said to him, Todd responded, "He asked me if I wanted to stay there or come back to you." Then, looking at his mother, he said, "I wanted to be with you and come home."[7]

7. THE GREAT SPIRIT: BLACK ELK'S NEAR DEATH EXPERIENCE

Black Elk, a Native American of the Lakota Sioux nation, lived between 1863 and 1950. Born on the Little Powder River in Montana, he died on a reservation in South Dakota. As a boy of nine, Black Elk collapsed with severe, painful swelling of his face, arms and legs. As he lost consciousness, he recounts that he was called by two men from the clouds, who said, "Hurry up, your grandfather is calling you." Black Elk was raised out of his tipi into the clouds, but felt sorry to leave his parents. In an even more dramatic encounter, he was told to behold the design in a classic Native American mandala: "the circular hoop, the four directions, and the center of the world on an axis stretching from sky to earth, neighing, dancing horses surrounded by lightning and thunder filled the sky at each direction." He was to follow a bay horse, which led him to a rainbow door, and inside were six grandfathers, "older than men can ever be – old like hills, old like stars."

The oldest grandfather welcomed him and said, "Your grandfathers all over the world are having a council, and they have called you here to teach you." Black Elk was frightened, he said, and knew that these were not old men, but "the Powers of the World." The first five grandfathers gave him the power to heal, the power of cleansing, the power of awakening and its peace, the power of growth, the power of transcendent vision, and the sixth grandfather grew backwards into youth until he became the youth, Black Elk.

The Great Spirit

The sixth grandfather then said, "My boy, have courage, for my power shall be yours, and you shall need it, for your nation on the earth will have great troubles." Black Elk received his powers from the six grandfathers and was sent back to his dying body. When he awoke, his parents told him he had been sick twelve days. Afraid to tell anyone of his visions until he was about seventeen, he finally told a medicine man who helped him to re-enact the vision as ritual, and immediately he became a power healer. The great sadness of his life was that he was not able to slow the influx of settlers from the East, or to stop the destructive power of industrial culture that nearly destroyed his people.[8]

UNPLEASANT OR HELL-LIKE NDES

P.M.H. Atwater, an important NDE researcher, collected 700 NDE cases and found that 105 were reports of negative, frightening or "hellish" experiences. This is a different finding from those of most earlier researchers. Before Atwater, most believed that only about 1%-3% of NDEs were distressing, but her conclusions are in line with more recent assessments by other people. [9] Also, this is an important issue as Gallup found that about 60% of Americans believe in hell.[10]

Atwater lists characteristics of frightening NDEs:

Lifeless or Threatening Apparitions
Barren or Ugly Expanses
Threats, Screams, Silence
Danger and the Possibility of Violence, Torture
Feelings of Cold or Extreme Temperatures

8. VASUDEV PANDEY

People from religious traditions other than Christian have both frightening and pleasant NDEs. For example, Osis and Haraldsson found that 14% of Indian Christians had frightening NDEs but 29% of Indian Hindus had them.[11]

Pandey is Hindu, and had this NDE in his home. He had been thought dead, and was actually taken to the cremation ground. After seeing signs of life, someone took him to a hospital where he was unconscious for three days. This experience was narrated in 1975: "Two persons caught me and took me with them. I felt tired after walking some distance: they started to drag me." He describes seeing a man, all black, who was not wearing any clothes, and was in a rage. He said to the attendants who had brought Pandey, "I had asked you to bring Vasudev the gardener. Our garden is drying up. You have brought Vasudev the student." When he regained consciousness, Pandey saw Vasudev the gardener standing in front of him, appearing healthy. People started to tease the gardener, saying, "Now it is your turn." The next morning Vasudev the gardener was dead. Pandey added that the "black man" had a club and used foul language, and Pandey called him Yamraj, the Hindu god of the dead. He also said that he was "brought back" by the same two men who had originally taken him to Yamraj.[12]

9. HANDSHAKE WITH THE GRIM REAPER

One of Atwater's cases is that of Gloria Hipple. Taken to the hospital due to a miscarriage, she was placed at a forty five degree angle because of bleeding, but the doctor who was supposed to care for her never arrived. After eight days (this is almost unbelievable) she says that she could not see and had a body temperature of 87.6 degrees.

"I recall being pulled down into a spinning vortex," she says, and felt drawn downward, head-first. She grabbed at the sides of the vortex, and thought of her children, then pleaded, "Please, not now..." but she kept moving. She tried to see something, but "...all there was to see was this cyclonic void that tapered into a funnel." She saw a black spot, "...like a dark curtain, falling in front of me." Then she saw a white dot, like a bright light at the end of a funnel, but as she came closer, it was a small white skull. "It became larger, grinning at me with bare sockets and gaping mouth, and traveling straight toward me like a baseball." She was terrified, and at first pleaded, "My baby is so little." Then she screamed, "No! damn it, no! Let me go. No! No! No! No!"

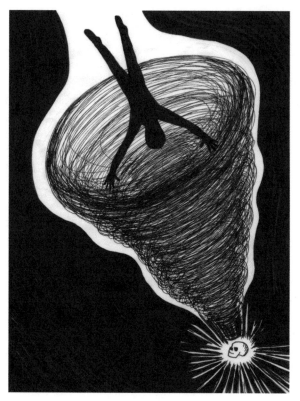

Handshake with the Grim Reaper

The skull shattered into fragments, and a bright white light came in place of the skull, a welcoming, peaceful light. She felt peace of mind, and felt herself floating upward, and immediately was back (in her body).

She heard her husband calling, and two doctors arrived. Taken to the operating room, she received several pints of blood and a week later was released.

She says that no one would believe her "...handshake with the grim reaper." Everyone laughed including her husband. "It was," she says, "the most horrendous, yet the most gratifying experience I've ever had in my life." (13)

10. THEY WERE LAUGHING AND SCREAMING

Atwater also tells an especially frightening story of a Virginia woman, Sandra Brock. She recounts that she had a stomach stapling, and during the same process, had a spleen removed. There was a great deal of hemorrhaging and the doctors expected that she would not survive. After the surgery and during one of the transfusions, she says, "I started feeling really weird. I felt like if I shut my eyes I would never open them again." She started being pulled through a tunnel, and in the tunnel, "...all I could see were people from my past..." She says there were people who were already dead, but who had in some way hurt her. "They were laughing and screaming, until I thought I could not stand it." She begged to be allowed to go back (to life) and could see a light at the end of a tunnel. But before she reached the light, she says, "All of a sudden I was back in bed, just thankful I had not died." This event has more than a flavor of mortality about it.(14)

PLEASANT OR HEAVEN-LIKE NDES

11. I FELT BETTER THAN I HAD EVER FELT IN MY LIFE

One of Kenneth Ring's cases involves Craig, a man in his late twenties, whose NDE included many more of the classic elements than most NDEs. This is a summary of Ring's long interview with Craig.

Craig had been rafting, when his inner tube pulled him to the middle of the river, where there was a waterfall. The current was powerful, and there was a suction hole at the bottom of the falls. Craig fell in headfirst. The water separated him from the tube, and pinned him to the bottom. Not surprisingly, at that point he realized that he would die, and as the air supply in his lungs had dwindled, "Scenes from my life began to pass before my eyes at super-high speeds," he said, and he felt like a passive observer, as if someone else was running a projector. He says, "I was looking at my life objectively for the first time ever. I saw the good as well as the bad." He saw himself sitting in a baby's highchair, and at a lake on a summer vacation when he was a little older. He remembered throwing his brother's air-bubble into the lake when he was angry, and remembers his father telling him that it was not nice to do what he did. His father told him that he would have to apologize, and go in the boat with his father to get the air bubble back. There were many images, particularly of experiences he had either learned from or were traumatic in some way.

A tingling sensation began at his feet and moved upward, and he became more relaxed. He felt himself moving into a dark void. "It was like a tunnel but it was so dark that it could have been five feet in diameter or thousands of miles." His speed increased, and he felt as if a wind was blowing across his face. Far away he saw a "...small pinpoint of light that seemed to be growing larger." As he moved closer, it became a "...huge mass of beautiful and brilliant white light." The light slowly engulfed him and he felt as if he had become one with the light. "I seemed to have knowledge of everything there is to know, and it accepted me as part of it." Everything seemed to make sense, and to be in total harmony.

Looking back, Craig says that he is still not able to explain the questions that were answered, or even the answers. It was as if there were a much higher level of thought. "I felt myself expand through the light over an area that seemed like miles..." He says, "I felt better than I had ever felt in my life. It was as if I was bathing in total love..." He had the sense that he had been there before, perhaps before he was born. Maybe Craig tasted the "unbidden flying rapture" mentioned by the novelist, Joseph Conrad in his short story, *Heart of Darkness.*

At this point, the out-of-body component began, and he floated up above the water, where he could hear the sound of the waterfall, and knew where his body was – eight feet under. But "...after experiencing such bliss and harmony, it seemed like everything prior to this was like being in some sort of cage." He says that he felt like an energy form that could never be destroyed, and realized that when handicapped people die, all their physical limitations would be cast aside, and they would feel whole again. He said he felt profound reassurance over this awareness. The events might seem to readers to be incomprehensible, but the emotions seem in themselves a special creation.

As Craig was in this euphoria, an old and partially transparent man came to inform him that he had a choice as to whether to return to life. He was shown what would happen if he chose to die, or to move on into the experience. The man also asked Craig what he had liked in life. When he said he had liked music, the man asked if he had done everything with music that he wanted to. Then the figure spoke of love and cooperation, and how the world could be a better place to life if people could see their importance. Craig realized that he really wanted to go back, to live his life to its fullest. "I said 'Okay,' but before I could get out the words. "I'm ready,' I shot back into my body like a lightning bolt." The final details of the rescue are not given in Ring's account.[15]

12. MEBRUKE: A MUSLIM NEAR DEATH EXPERIENCE

Mebruke is a Saudi Arabian woman who at the age of twenty was swimming in the Mediterranean off the coast of Italy. She became tired, headed for shore, but slipped beneath the waves. As she went under for the fourth time, she tells that she was no longer aware of her body, but saw a beautiful light. It was bright, but had a profoundly calming effect. She attempts to explain:

Mebruke

"In my religion there are beings called angels who are made out of pure white light. Maybe that is what I saw." Then Mebruke heard a voice, "You are not to die like this." Suddenly, she said, she felt "an energy" shoot from her feet to her head, and she was "propelled out of the water," as though someone was physically lifting her, but she says, "I can swear that there was no physical being there." She was "moved through the water," and shortly a boat arrived and a man pulled her out. In a lighthearted way, she says, "When he did that, I started to laugh because I was so glad to be out of the water."[16]

13. FRANK: A MELANESIAN NEAR DEATH EXPERIENCE

Melanesia is a group of hundreds of islands in the South Pacific, to the north and east of Australia. Frank, suffering from an apparently fast-moving infection which began in his leg, believed he was dying and asked to be taken to the beach and placed under a lean-to. He reports that he believes he died for about five minutes, but then saw a group of ancestor spirits who showed him a road. As he followed it, he saw a man "with white skin and long white robes, a beard and long hair." He was "bright" as though a flashlight focused on him, and the light seemed to be directed toward Frank. The man held his hands toward Frank, palms up, blocking the road. Then the man moved a finger to motion Frank to stop, then to turn around, and come back.

Frank then says Alois, (who had died some time before) cut his leg and spit ginger on it, and he saw a group of men dancing and singing. One old man, whose name was Kasiru, said, "Who do you think did this to you?" But the other men scolded him for poisoning Frank, and they made a song which had in it the words, Kasiru, and "knee is tight." Frank apparently recovered, and says that "When I came to myself, I remembered the song and have taught it to others." [17]

14. I REFUSED

M.W., a grandmother from Ohio and Hospice volunteer tells this story. "I became sick at my mother's funeral, and at one point it felt like someone was pressing a dull table knife into my abdomen, so I went to lie down for a few minutes. My stomach was like a Mix Master. Then I don't remember anything from that point on until about 1:30 a.m. when I must have fallen out of bed in the hospital. I must have been picked up, and I knew that several doctors and nurses were gathered around me, trying to get a blood pressure, but there was none. If they had asked me to move my hand, I couldn't have done it . I remember being on the floor, then all of a sudden it was like headlights in a fog, very bright, but not like hospital lights. I thought 'Whoa! I'm in deep trouble. But I can't go (into death). My husband, my children, my grandchildren, and we've just buried Mom – I can't go.' I had a perforated bowel and septic shock, which usually kills, and several doctors told me they didn't know how I survived. I was in the hospital thirty days, but I just wasn't ready to leave my family, and I refused to go."

15. A BEAUTIFUL AND GLORIOUS MOMENT

One of Moody's cases involved a young woman who had recently had a difficult delivery of a child. She had lost considerable blood, and the doctor had told her relatives that she was dying. "Yet," she says, "I was quite alert through the whole thing..." and felt herself coming to as he was saying this.

Then, "As I did, I realized that all these people were there, almost in multitudes..." gathered near the ceiling of the room. She recognized them as people whom she had known but who had passed on. "I recognized my grandmother and a girl I had known when I was in school, and many other relatives and friends." She saw their faces and felt their presence, and says that all of them seemed pleased. It was to her like a homecoming, a happy occasion, and they seemed to be there to protect or guide her. "All this time, I had the feeling of everything light and beautiful. It was a beautiful and glorious moment." [18]

16. THAT IS WHEN I WAS BORN AGAIN

One of Atwater's cases is of thirty seven year-old Jeannine Wolff, who nearly died following complications related to endometriosis. Yet there is a tranquil dignity about her experience. "Suddenly I was aware of being in the most beautiful garden I've ever seen. I felt whole and loved." She heard "celestial music" and saw vivid, unearthly colors, of flowers and trees. "As I looked around, I saw at a distance, on a hill, Jesus Christ." Jesus said to her that it was her choice whether to come back to earth, and she chose to come back to finish her work. "That is when I was born again." Describing the changes in her life, she believes she is more aware of people's needs, feelings, and beliefs, and is more compassionate and considerate. She also is more confident of God's love.[19]

17. RESTORING A SOUL

One of Ring's cases is of Peggy, who says, "...my consciousness must have pulled away from my body because I suddenly observed it from a short distance as it sobbed." She was completely unemotional as she observed her body, and, "As I watched, I saw some shiny, clear object lift away from my body. It was obvious to me it was my ego." This sense of losing oneself is a goal of spiritual practices in most religious traditions, but she did not want her ego to leave her, being unfamiliar with the vast mystical literature. She felt that she had to have it in order to be alive. As the ego pulled away, she says, "...I saw in it all the things I had done wrong in my life." She was stunned, thinking that the ego was part of her and could not be separated. "I can't tell you how happy I was when it dawned on me that 'that was never me.'"

Peggy began to realize that she was not only okay without it, but better off. "It was sort of like taking a dusty, old, clogged up, used filter off an air-conditioner vent..." Instead of air going through an air-conditioner vent, "...it was pure undiluted love going through me." In this exquisite brilliance, as she relaxed and allowed the light to pour energy into her, she began to feel like she deserved that magnificent energy. "If there is such a thing as 'restoring a soul,' then that's exactly what happened to me." [20]

18. LIKE A MAN WITH A PARACHUTE

Ian Currie cites a case of Kenneth G., who gives one of the most emotional and detailed NDE descriptions of an environment. He must have felt possessed by eternity. Kenneth was resuscitated after a cardiac arrest. Apparently he was not happy to be back, and said so to those around his bedside. "When I go again, please leave me alone," he said. And yet the whole story throws a special kind of light on our study of the NDE.

"I found myself in the most enchanting place you could ever visit," he said. He describes it as a beauty far beyond anything he had ever seen, a luxuriant wide valley, sloping down from gentle rolling hills. "There is no way to express to you the intense enjoyment I felt with the place..." he says, and that he was '...floating down, very slowly like man with a parachute." Drifting out of the sky, he landed in a field of high grass, and saw that the meadow "...went on forever." In the middle of the field, he could see animals, flowers and trees, and says, in a kind of exquisite excitability, "I'd never seen anything like the profusion of beautiful growing plants and flowers in this place."

After listening to the sound of the rustling of grass, Kenneth says that he heard a voice calling him, and soon recognized it as the voice of his deceased father. Apparently quite astonished, he thought, "What is he doing here?" The voice kept saying, "Kenneth, don't be afraid. Do not worry, I have come to help you with your journey."

Then he heard laughter, and saw children playing in an amusement park, which looked like a park he had played in as a child. His childhood playmates were there, looking just like they had looked sixty years earlier, but none noticed him. Kenneth felt, "...I was a little boy again, reliving [my] youth ...God it was beautiful!" He thought that death had blended the hereafter with his fondest childhood memories, and the report ends with "How wrong for them to bring me back from such a wonderful...place." [21]

VERIFIABLE NDES

Verifiable NDEs are those in which the subject gives a report about what she has seen during the NDE, in a place where it was physically impossible for her to have been, that turns out to be **verified.** These are like the higher level OBEs described in Chapter Five, except that these events happen in people near death.

19. THE LOOK ON THE SURGEON'S FACE

An Australian correspondent reports: "I will never forget the look on the surgeon's face when (after surgery) I told him that I went through the OBE (out-of-body) phenomenon during the operation." She then asked the surgeon whether he was sitting on a green stool with a white top on it. He said he was, but then said, in one of those common but mysterious denials, "But you could not have seen that from where you were lying on the operating table." She told him that she did not see it from where she was lying, but had seen it from above during the OBE, and said, "This remark caused an even stranger look on his face." [22]

20. NURSE VAN WYK

A South African, in describing his NDE, said, "While I was in a coma (and I believe clinically dead), my friend, the nurse was killed in an automobile accident. I met her on the Other Side." Nurse Van Wyk asked him to return, he said, promised that he would meet a loving wife, and asked him to tell her parents she loved them and was sorry she had wrecked her birthday present. Nurse Van Wyk had apparently received a red car, an MGB, from her parents. Then the patient told the nursing staff upon his return that he knew Nurse Van Wyk had been killed and the car she was killed in was a red MGB. The information about the red MGB was apparently known only by Nurse Van Wyk's parents. After this information was given, the patient said, rather triumphantly, "...people started to sit up and take notice." [23]

21. I SAW YOUR YELLOW SMOCK

A clinical nursing instructor was helping in the emergency room to resuscitate a man who had died. The medics were shocking him, Ms. Saunders was trying to give him oxygen, and in the middle of the resuscitation someone took over for her and she left. Several days later, she met the patient, who spontaneously said, "You looked so much better in your yellow smock." More than a little surprised, Ms. Saunders had in fact been wearing a yellow smock that day. The patient commented further, as though more evidence was needed: "Yea, I saw you. You had something over my face, and you were pushing air into me. I saw your yellow smock." Ms. Saunders reports, "This really gave me the chills! The only way he would have known that information was if he was there and alert/conscious /or out-of-body." Then, "It's really uncanny to think that he remembered a color! I would never have believed it if I had not been part of this." [24]

22. WELL YES, THESE THINGS ARE TRUE

One of Moody's earliest cases is rather low-key, and involved a young person who reports that when she woke after the accident, she did not really want to know what shape she was in, or what the doctors were predicting concerning her recovery. She only wanted to talk about the incomprehensible experience she had been through. She correctly informed her father of the identity of the person who had dragged her body out of the building, even what color of clothes that person was wearing, how they had rescued her, and even the conversation that was being held among the rescuers. Then she said, "And my father said, 'Well yes, these things are true.'" Yet, she insists, her body was "out" the whole time, that there was no way she could have known these things without being outside her body.[25]

LIFE CHANGING NDES

Almost all NDE have a profound effect on those who have them, and even on those who only hear of them. These cases have especially striking outcomes.

23. THIS IS A COMMITMENT BETWEEN MYSELF AND THE LIGHT

Kenneth Ring describes the events surrounding Mart Chandler's profound life change. Chandler had his first NDE in 1964, when almost nothing was known of NDEs. Both his wife and his mother had hard-minded and rather negative reactions when he told them, so he kept it to himself. Even the discovery of Moody's work in 1977 did not change their attitudes, but about ten years later Chandler attended a presentation by Raymond Moody. He shared his experience with Moody and several other experiencers, and their validation had "a profound effect" according to Chandler. Before long, as though lit by a sacred fire, he was speaking publicly about his experience and discovered Ring's book *Heading Toward Omega*, which documents the long-term impact of NDEs. He wrote a paper then on the impact of the NDE, with special emphasis on the life changes and insights he gained. "During the experience," he says, "I made a definite statement to the Light that I had to accomplish important things when I came back." And "I feel that I must do the very best I can while I am here."

Chandler lists ways that his NDE changed him. His self esteem improved, and so he was able to become more socially involved. He gained a desire to help others, with more compassion, empathy, patience and more of an ability to express love and acceptance of others as they are. Brought up a Catholic, he moved away from "orthodox" religion, but gained a deeper feeling about the existence of God, especially about God as a God of love, compassion, and forgiveness. He has moved away from ideas of "...a God of retribution and infinite punishment." His quest for spiritual values has increased "severalfold" and his fear of death diminished. He also found an increase in a psychic ability to have "advanced knowledge of future events." [26]

24. SHE REALLY WANTED TO SAY, "YOU'VE GONE CRAZY."

One of Moody's cases is of a rather harsh man with a crusty sense of humor. "When I 'came back,' no one knew quite what to make of me." He describes himself as an angry, driven, "type A" kind of person. "If things didn't go right for me, I was impossible to live with. That was at home as well as at work." He had a heart attack, and an NDE, and reflecting back says, "Why she (his wife) put up with it, I don't know." He thought perhaps she had grown accustomed to it, because after his NDE "...she could hardly put up with my mellowness." He says that he didn't yell at her any more, or push her to do things, and says, "I became the easiest person to live with and the change was almost more than she could bear." He claims that it took a great deal of patience on HIS part to keep the marriage together! "She kept saying, 'You are so different since your heart attack.' I think she really wanted to say, 'You've gone crazy.' " [27]

25. A BENIGN VIRUS

One of the findings in the research is that those who ONLY HEAR of the NDE show life changes nearly as impressive as those who have DIRECTLY experienced it. Between 1985 and 1994 at the University of Connecticut, Kenneth Ring was teaching psychology, and sharing some of his research on the NDE. At the end of the semesters, he asked questions of the students in some of his classes. He found that 96% were more convinced of the authenticity of NDEs, 61% became more spiritually oriented, and 71% said their ideas about God had changed. **None** reported that their belief in God had weakened. Here are statements that show students' responses to the courses, which in turn led Ring to call the NDE "A Benign Virus." These changes are also supported by other studies in other countries.

"I have become more spiritual and it has also reinforced my beliefs about the unimportance or wealth and material objects."

"I have less fear of death ...(and) am more spiritual."

"What I have gained from studying the NDE this semester: (1) more concern for all people; (2) less fear of the ending of this life; (3) more open-mindedness to learn as much as I can while I still can."

"What I have gained most from studying NDEs is that love is the driving force of all humanity, I have re-evaluated my beliefs about God, reincarnation, and spirituality in that my belief in them is stronger. I felt that, with this course, I have grown as a person."

"A more spiritual view of myself and the world. The understanding of what is REALLY [her capitalization] important in life, and a break from some of the materialistic values that I had." [28]

26. A THEOLOGICAL STUDENT REFLECTS

"My doctor told me I 'died' during the surgery, but I told him that I came to life." This must have been an immense experience, for he continued with candor, "I saw in that vision what a stuck-up ass I was, ...looking down on everyone who wasn't a member of my denomination." Further, he said, "A lot of people I know are going to be surprised when they find out that the Lord isn't interested in theology." He believes the Lord finds denominationalism amusing. "He wanted to know what was in my **heart**, not my **head**." [29]

27. THE VIRUS SPREADS

Another of Ring's cases is a report by a man who only heard about the NDE. "NDEs have greatly reduced any fear of death I had. In fact they've eliminated it." He goes on to say that NDEs have enriched his spiritual life by helping to move it out of the mystical and into a more direct, or personal, way of seeing things. For him, NDEs clarified spiritual concepts, like reincarnation, and the life review. "They have brought these out as something real, and not just something hoped for and presented to us as theological theories..." He feels that the primacy of love as a Living Force has been enhanced, and is the meaning and goal of all actions and all things. They (NDEs) have also strengthened his belief that "...what is truly spiritual goes far beyond the beliefs and restrictions of any and all religions...." [30]

28. A MAJOR LIFE CHANGE

A retired professor took the time to study and ponder the literature on NDEs, and it brought about, he said, "a major life change." As a person who had for some time been searching for answers to existential questions, he had read scientific and philosophical books, but says, "...they left my heart as unsatisfied as ever." After reading Moody's first book, *Life After Life,* he was struck not so much by Moody's analysis as by the testimonies of the experiencers. This was more than a sentimental revival. "I read, cried a lot, and knew it was true!" he said. He was touched at a level other than the intellectual, where he had spent most of his life. "I had the impression that this was a truth I had always known, but had simply forgotten. Yes, it was a revelation – and a relief." [31]

29. MILLIONS UPON MILLIONS FEARED DEATH

One NDEer is clearly on a mission: "I decided I had to tell what I had learned about this magnificent domain," she said. "Millions upon millions feared death. Wouldn't they be glad to know that only the body dies..." And finally, "I wanted to shout what I'd learned from the housetops, share it with all the people of the world." [32]

DISCUSSION

LESS THAN PLEASANT REPORTS

Unpleasant or "hellish" reports of NDEs are troubling to many people. One researcher, a cardiologist named Maurice Rawlings, found a large number of cases in which people gave initial descriptions of "hell" but then he says the reports became "heaven-like" as events progressed. He believes people mostly remember the "heaven-like" events after they are revived. Rawlings goes on to say that if people want to avoid the horrors of hell they must commit themselves to the doctrines of Christianity.

No other researcher has produced this large number of such frightening accounts, or interpreted them in such a judgmental way. So his cases may well be products of his work in a particular location, Chattanooga, TN, and/ or with a particular group of fundamentalist Christians. Except for Rawlings' work, the research on NDEs does not support the belief in everlasting torment held by many Christians. Because of this, we have not included his cases in this account.

Nevertheless, some non-fundamentalist people have described frightening NDEs as "hellish." Such reports bring to mind for many people the common idea of hell as a place of unremitting and unending punishment. Careful study of the Hebrew Scriptures and the New Testament shows that what came to be translated as hell was in fact an Aramaic word referring to the **city dump**, where trash was burned, and the word also suggests mental torment and regret. Long before the development of Christian theology, there were common beliefs in an abode of the dead, and ideas about everlasting torment. Nearly every idea of punishment - hell, sheol, gehenna, suggested in the Old and New Testaments is paralleled in other and older literature. The writers of the Hebrew Scriptures and the New Testament were drawing on ideas from Semitic folklore. These came from Mesopotamian and Canaanitic literature, Iranian Ivestan teachings, and from Egypt, Greece and Rome far more than from Hebrew ideas.[33]

Some Greek philosophers, before the Christian era, even wrote that they believed ideas of eternal punishment were useful to keep citizens obedient to their governments. Some critics believe that the church then took over a practice that worked for the pagans and used it to keep converts obedient to the church.[34]

Negative NDE reports raise the question of the ultimate fate of persons such as Hitler. Ring finds that the Life Review includes the **experiencing** of the pain one has inflicted on others, **for the full length of time those others were afflicted.** For this reason Ring and others rightly talk about the educational value of the NDE.

In any event, ideas of heaven, hell and even purgatory in the various religious traditions are very likely related to actual reports people have given through the centuries of NDEs.

NDES AS HALLUCINATIONS?

Most skeptics of life after death hold the view that all NDEs can be explained as hallucinations related to oxygen starvation in the brain, or drug reactions, or results of psychological problems. Here we will comment on the scientific issues in the hallucination argument.

One philosopher of science points out that, indeed, some apparent NDEs are best explained as hallucinations. But apparent NDEs of this sort, given a closer look, will prove to be very different from NDEs in the richer reports. For instance, one apparent NDEer saw a red light, almost unheard of in NDE research. Then he tried unsuccessfully to communicate with "two creatures" about how the universe needed to be "put right." It turns out that in other important ways also, his "NDE" was very different from the cases presented in this chapter.

Also, hallucinations of mental patients do not show any of the consistency and pattern that the better NDEs demonstrate, nor do the hallucinations of oxygen starved patients. Researchers do admit that certain drugs, such as ketamine or LSD (lysergic acid diethylomide) can trigger out of body sensations and a sense of being in a tunnel. But these characteristics are not, by themselves, seriously offered as evidence of the NDE really being what it appears to be – something actually leaving the body.[35]

In our judgment, the veridical cases, in which the NDE person reports independently verified information, the similarity of thousands of cases, their consistent differences from drug or emotionally related events, and the profound life changes following NDEs are the best evidence that NDEs should be taken seriously. To many people, they clearly suggest that the NDE is indeed a glimpse of another level of existence outside of the physical body, and that life after the death of the body is possible.

FOOTNOTES

1. Cited by Raymond Moody, *The Light Beyond,* Bantam Books, New York, 1998, page 6.
2. Melvin Morse, *Closer To The Light,* Ivy Books, New York, 1990, pages 34-36.
3. Morse, *Ibid.,* pages 36-37.
4. Raymond Moody, *Op. Cit.* pages 61-62.
5. Robert Moss, "Through the Moongate," http://chicagoiands.org/stories/Robert%20 Moss, page 1.
6. From Russell Noyes, cited by Ian Currie, *You Cannot Die,* Somerville House, Toronto, 1998, pages 207-208.
7. Kenneth Ring, *Lessons From The Light,* Moment Point Press, Portsmouth, NH, 1998, pages 104-105..
8. "The Great Spirit: Black Elk's Near Death Experience" at http://www.near- death.com/ elk.html
9. P.M.H. Atwater, "Is There a Hell?" at http://www.cinemind.com/atwater/hell.html, pages 2-3.
10. Bruce Goldberg, "Near Death Experiences" at http://www.lightparty.com/Spirituality/ NearDeath.html, page 3.
11. Karlis Osis and Erlendur Haraldsson, *At The Hour Of Death,* Avon, New York, . 1977, page 89.
12. Satwant Pasricha and Ian Stevenson, "Near-Death Experiences of Hindus, http:// www.near-death.com/hindu.html, pages 1-2.
13. P.M.H. Atwater, *Beyond the Light,* Birch Lane Press, Seacaucus, NJ, 1995, pages 29-30.
14. *Ibid.,* pages 32-33.
15. Kenneth Ring, *Op. Cit.,* pages 12-16.
16. "Near-Death Experiences of Muslims" at http.//www.near-death.com/muslim.html
17. "Near-Death and Out-Of-Body Experiences in a Melanesian Society," by Dorothy E. Counts at http://watarts.uwaterloo.ca/ANTHRO/rwpark/WNB/NearDeath.html
18. Raymond Moody, *Life After Life,* Stackpole Press, Harrisburg, PA, 1976, page 53.
19. P. M. H. Atwater, *Op. Cit.,* page 46.
20. Kenneth Ring, *Op. Cit.,* pates 52-53.
21. Ian Currie, *Op. Cit.,* pages 211-212.
22. Kenneth Ring, *Op. Cit.,* page 59.
23. *Ibid.,* page 64.
24. *Ibid.,* pages 68-69.
25. Raymond Moody, *Op.Cit.,* page 95.
26. Kenneth Ring, *Op. Cit.,* pages 141-142.
27. Raymond Moody, *The Light Beyond.,* Bantam Books, New York, 1988, pages 51- 52.
28. Kenneth Ring, *Op. Cit.,* pages 208-209.
29. Raymond Moody, *The Light Beyond,* page 49.
30. Kenneth Ring, *Op. Cit.,* pages 209-210
31. *Ibid.,* page 211.
32. *Ibid.,* page 250.
33. See *The Interpreter's Dictionary of the Bible,* Abingdon Press, Nashville, 1962, pages 361-362, 787-788.
34. "Ancient and Modern Perpetrators of Hell" at http://www.what-the-hell-is-hell.com/ AncientHell.html
35. Robert Almeder, *Death and Personal Survival,* Littlefield Adams Quality Paperbacks, Lanham, MD, 1992, pages 174-183.

CHAPTER FOUR

DEATHBED VISIONS

"You have got to tell all the old people
so they won't be afraid to die."

> Chris, an eight year old who had
> an NDE at age four.
> (Morse, *Parting Visions*, Chapter 1)

Deathbed Visions are first cousins of NDEs, and refer to experiences reported by some terminally ill patients who then die without resuscitation. There are fewer studies of DBVs than of the other events that suggest life after death, but the studies we have are both qualitative and quantitative and so may be of more scientific interest to some readers. It is important to remember that these are not patients' reports, but reports of observers who describe the events. Most observers have no reason to fabricate or lie about this.

In *One Last Hug Before I Go: The Mystery and Meaning of Death Bed Visions,* Carla Wills-Brandon estimates that though only about 10% of people are conscious and able to describe their experiences, as many as 50% may in fact have DBVs before the death of their bodies. In many other patients, these experiences are "medicated away." Along with NDEs, it is likely that DBVs have through the centuries had a strong influence on ideas about an afterlife in the various religious traditions. There are especially well-documented reports of DBVs in adherents to Judaism, Hinduism, and Christianity.

In the most carefully done research on DBVs, Karlis Osis, Ph.D., at the American Society for Psychical Research, and Erlendur Haraldsson, Ph.D., an Icelandic psychologist, found that visions of friends, loved ones, and religious figures, and of heavenly environments were the most frequent reports. Related to these usually pleasant encounters, there were also medically unexplainable mood changes, usually in a positive direction. Melvin Morse, M.D., and Carla Wills-Brandon, Ph.D., have also focused on the deeply moving DBVs that have a profound emotional impact on surviving loved ones. Examples follow of these four types of DBVs.

The most striking cases may be those verifiable cases in which the patient saw someone in a vision who had in fact died, but whose death was unknown to the patient. Other cases involve visitors at the bedside who "see" the deceased loved ones whom the patient also reports seeing. This variety of cases is presented according to four major themes. In other chapters, e.g. Chapter Five, they are ordered by the strength of the verifiability.

SEEING DECEASED LOVED ONES AND RELIGIOUS FIGURES

1. WHY PAPA! YOU DIDN'T TELL ME!

This well-documented case involves two American girls, Jennie and Edith, both age eight. It is a bitter-sweet kind of report. Both had caught diphtheria, and Jennie died. Edith was so sick that her parents decided not to tell her of the death of Jennie, her best friend. Before Edith died, she must have stunned her family when she appeared to be seeing people who had predeceased her. Surprised, she turned to her father and said, "Why Papa! I'm going to take Jennie with me! ...You did not tell me that Jennie was here." [1]

2. DON'T WORRY, I'LL TAKE CARE OF THE BABY

A young woman, Maxine, had given birth to a baby in Anaheim, California. While resting, she was surprised to see her father standing in an upper corner of the room holding a baby in his arms. He said, "Don't worry. I'll take care of the baby," then he disappeared. Suspicious and concerned, Maxine asked the nurse how the baby was, and was told that the baby was doing fine. Maxine became more suspicious and demanded of her husband that he tell her the truth. We can barely conceive of the blow she must have felt when her husband told her that the baby had been stillborn, and that her father also had died suddenly after she had entered the hospital. Maxine had not been told of her father's death. [2]

3. IF YOU COULD SEE WHAT I DO, YOU WOULD KNOW I CAN'T STAY

After giving birth to a baby in England, Doris appeared to see something in one corner of the room, and smiled. "Oh lovely, lovely," she said. Asked what she saw, she reported "Lovely brightness - wonderful beings." Then, with joy, she said, "Why, it's Father! Oh, he's so glad I'm coming. ..." Her baby was brought for her to see, and after looking at it, she surprised everyone: she asked, "Do you think I ought to stay for baby's sake?" Then she turned again toward the vision and said, "...I can't stay. If you could see what I do, you'd know I can't stay." She turned to her husband and asked him, "You won't let baby go with anyone who won't love him, will you?" Then, "Let me see the lovely brightness..." All this is astonishing enough, but then she spoke to her father, "I'm coming," and to the doctor, "Oh, he is so near…," then "He has Vida with him…" Vida was Doris' sister, who had died two weeks earlier. Because of her own serious heart condition during pregnancy, Doris had not been told of Vida's death before she died.[3]

4. "COMING TO THE END OF A LIFE SPENT DYING"

One of Melvin Morse's cases involved Cory, a seven year old who had been diagnosed with leukemia at age three. It is a tragic story: Cory had suffered four relapses since the diagnosis, and each had been more difficult to treat, and Cory wanted to stop treatment. Of course this presented a dilemma for his physicians, and for Morse himself who was consulted on the case.

Disappointed, and falling asleep on the way home from the hospital after learning of his last bone marrow relapse, Cory woke up and told his mother, "Don't worry about my leukemia. I have been to the crystal castle and have talked with God." He said that he had traveled up a beam of light and crossed a rainbow bridge to visit the crystal castle. He said that he "felt good" and that God had engulfed him in a "loving light."

There were many visions after this, striking in themselves, but this stunning event also happened. Cory told his mother that in one of his visions he met an old boyfriend of hers who had been crippled in an auto accident. His mother had never told Cory of the man, and had not seen him for many years. But Cory, after one of his visits to the crystal castle, told her that a man had approached him and introduced himself as an old boy-friend of his mother's, and said that he had been unable to walk for many years. "Don't worry now, Mom," said Cory. "He said to tell you he can walk now. He's in the crystal castle."

On another occasion, Cory said that he saw one of his friends at the hospital while visiting the crystal castle. His mother thought that this was not likely since they had seen him at the hospital only a week before. But returning to the hospital for chemotherapy on the next day, they must have been dumbfounded to find that the young friend had unexpectedly died the night before.

On one occasion, Cory described God as an old man with a beard and a halo. This might not seem surprising to those who feel that deathbed visions are influenced by religious beliefs of parents and of the religion and culture surrounding the dying person. But in this case, the mother believed in reincarnation and karma, not in a Judeo-Christian male deity. Morse does not mention the father's or other family members' beliefs.

Finally, Cory said he was told by God that he should forgo any more chemotherapy, and died during the same week as he said God had told him that he would die.[4]

5. I'VE SEEN GOD, ANGELS AND SHEPHERDS

Another of Morse's heart-rending cases involved seven year old Seth. Seth was also dying of leukemia, and had been hospitalized for severe and untreatable pneumonia. Three days before he died, Seth suddenly sat up and announced that Jesus was in the room, and asked everyone to pray for him. This must have been a sad but tender moment for those in the room with him. Then later, Seth again sat up and said, "There are beautiful colors in the sky. There are beautiful colors and more colors. You can double jump up here, double jump!" And later, even though his breathing was difficult and his heart pounding, he said to his parents, "…let me go. …Don't be afraid. I've seen God, angels, and shepherds. I see the white horse." Then, "It's wonderful. It's beautiful."

In another striking detail of the case, Seth's housebound aged grandmother said she saw a vision of Seth asking her to come to the hospital. Though she had not been out of her house in ten years, with tender affection for her grandson, she called a taxi and struggled to the hospital to see him. Though she knew before the vision that he was in the hospital, Morse thinks the timing of Seth's powerful visions, her vision, and her visit may have been more than coincidence.[5]

6. I AM GOING TO THE LAND OF GOD

According to a health care worker, a Hindu woman, dying of diabetes, kept uttering words, and the worker listened at the request of the relatives of the patient. The patient said that her mother, who had died many years earlier, had come, calling her to accompany her to the "land of God." When the health care worker told this to the relatives, they were distressed as they considered it a bad omen, and asked her to tell the patient not to go. With a mind of her own, the patient said she was going and seemed happy, saying, "I am going; mother is calling me. I am going to the land of God." These were her last words, and the health care worker notes that before this experience, the patient had expected to recover. This kind of case argues against the theory held by some psychologically oriented skeptics, that deathbed visions are examples of wish fulfillment as a psychological defense mechanism.[6]

7. HAPPY TO SEE THOSE GODS

Another Hindu patient was suffering from a liver disease. He was receiving no sedatives, had a slight fever, but appeared confused and had difficulty responding to questions. He did seem to be aware of other people who were present. Though he initially was not ready to die, now he told how he felt himself to be flying into another world, where he saw gods sitting and calling him. He seemed to want to go, and asked the people in the room to "Go away from me, I am dying." He had the visions again of the gods, and insisted that it was not a hallucination but a true experience. He argued that this was the world he wanted to live in, and was no longer concerned about dying. According to the health worker's report, he looked better, and felt elated about his experience, and died shortly afterward.[7]

8. REASSURANCE FROM THE PATIENT TO THE SURVIVOR
Carla Wills-Brandon gives a case in which an elderly woman had a serious stroke and was unconscious for a few days. Her nephew's wife was visiting her, and the wife had lost a daughter a year earlier. The patient's nephew's wife kindly asked her (deceased) daughter to come to visit the patient. The patient suddenly came out of her coma, and wanted to talk about the dead daughter. She said she had seen the daughter, that she looked beautiful, that she was safe and with God. Then, stunned, the patient's nephew's wife said that she was so surprised that the patient had mentioned her daughter, because she had lost many other people who were much closer to her.[8]

9. YOU LOOK WELL AND WELL-CARED FOR
A sixty-nine year old woman was dying of cancer, but according to the health care person, was not receiving any drugs. With a very soft voice, and a smile on her face, the patient seemed to be in conversation with her deceased husband, telling him how much she loved him, how she missed him and how she would join him. "It won't be long now before I'm with you," she said, and reaching out as if she felt his hand, "You look well and well cared for." [9]

10. A NURSE ALSO SEES THE APPARITIONS OF THE VISITORS
This well-known case involves a nurse, Joy Snell, who was caring for a seventeen year old patient, Laura Stirman, who was also a personal friend. Laura was dying of tuberculosis and was in no pain, but suffered the typical extreme exhaustion. The nurse was also a psychic, and reports rather matter-of-factly.

Joy Snell reports that shortly before Laura died, she became aware of two spirit forms standing by the bedside of her patient. She says she did not see them enter the room, but that "…they were standing by the bedside when they first became visible to me…." She tells that she could see them as distinctly as any of the human occupants of the room, and she recognized their faces as close friends of the girl who was dying. These friends had

47

A nurse also sees the apparition of the visitors.

passed away a year before, and had been about the same age as the patient. Since the nurse and the patient were friends, we may assume that the nurse knew of the deaths of the friends before seeing the "spirit forms." [10]

SEEING HEAVEN-LIKE ENVIRONMENTS

According to Osis and Haraldsson's findings, after the experience of seeing deceased loved ones and religious figures, seeing heaven-like environments was the most common report by dying patients. Other researchers do not seem to find or report as many of these heavenly environment cases, probably because there actually are far fewer of them.

11. A TAXI TO HEAVEN?

An educated eighty year old woman was suffering from cardiac failure. Four days before she died, she was listless, but alert, and her temperature and pulse were normal. She told the health care worker that a taxi driver had driven her to a lovely garden, where she saw, beautiful flowers and "endless gardens..." It was gorgeous, she said, and said she had never seen anything like it. She didn't want to leave, but the taxi driver, less appreciative and feeling that he was wasting time, was anxious to get started. She complained

A taxi to heaven

that he got lost and took too long getting home, but that she would gladly go back there any day, and that it was a "beautifully done garden." [11]

12. TECHNOLOGICAL GRANDEUR

Technological grandeur is Osis and Haraldsson's fine title for this Irish patient's vision. A nurse said that he suddenly had a glow about his face, then said, "…you know these wonderful things they are doing today, all the Sputniks and all those rocket things up there." He seemed to be happy, then said, "I was up there and they did not let me in." The nurse said, "…that glow – it was almost like a trance. It was very strange." [12]

13. A VERY MEAN NASTY PERSON

A healthcare worker described an attitude conversion in a seventy eight year old patient, She was, she said "…always nasty, a very mean person." Then, she reports, the patient called her to see how lovely and beautiful heaven is. Then, "… she looked at me and seemed surprised: 'Oh, but you can't see it, you aren't here [in heaven], you are over there.' " [13]

14. A GREAT SUNSET, YOU KNOW

A nurse reported that her patient said, "It looked like a great sunset, very large, you know, and beautiful. The clouds suddenly appeared to be gates."

This patient, like many others, became very serene, and said she was now ready to die.[14]

15. MY GOD, I THOUGHT I WAS IN HELL

The only case Osis and Haraldsson found of a "hellish" vision is as follows, though there were several reported from other researchers in the chapter on Near Death Experiences. The patient, very disturbed, said "I thought I was dead, I was in hell." Then, "My God, I thought I was in hell." She described the experience, and said that the devil would take her because of her sins, and because of what other people thought of her. According to the health care person, she had long standing guilt feelings and believed God was punishing her for her sins. Understandably, she became extremely frightened.

Osis and Haraldsson add that, if visions of this type are triggered by guilt, or by religious teachings, we might expect far more of them than we actually find.[15]

MEDICALLY UNEXPLAINABLE MOOD CHANGES

16. A VISION TRANSFORMED HER ENTIRE BEING

These are the words a medical professional used to describe the DBV that happened to a woman in her seventies. She was suffering from pneumonia, and was a semi-invalid who had, according to the reporter, "…spent a painful miserable existence." The caregiver writes, as though she herself was moved, "Her face became so serene, as if she had seen something beautiful. There was a transfixed illumination on her face – a smile beyond description." The serenity lasted until her death an hour later.[16]

17. HER *ATTITUDE* SEEMED TO HAVE CHANGED

A fifty nine year old woman had pneumonia with cardiac involvement. Her caretaker seems to have been stunned, and described the events this way: "The expression on her face was beautiful; her *attitude* seemed to have changed entirely. This was more than a change of the mood I had seen her in many times before…" The care giver felt that there was something not natural about the event, that "…there was something just a little beyond us," and noted that her presumed contact with the beyond had a happy effect on her. [17]

18. MRS. JONES, THIS WATER WILL SEE ME THROUGH THE JORDAN

Osis and Haraldsson think that **the strength to die gracefully comes from the feeling that another world exists.** In this case an elderly man with tuberculosis was dying, and his care giver reported, "His serenity was so sudden. One day he said to me, "Mrs. Jones, will you bring me a tall glass of water with lots of ice?" After drinking it, he said, "Mrs. Jones, this water will see me through the Jordan." He died ninety minutes later, and the doctors were surprised because there were no other signs of his imminent death.[18]

19. DISENGAGEMENT FROM PAIN

A fifty year old leukemia patient had been known to be cranky and frightened for the past several weeks. But apparently crankiness did not work well for him, since the care giver reported that, "As death was more imminent, he seemed to realize there was something more to life than just problems. He became more serene and thoughtful about those he would leave behind." [19]

IMPACT OF THE DBV ON SURVIVING LOVED ONES

20. IT WAS SO PEACEFUL TO WATCH HER PASS

A daughter tells of the death of her mother, and how the DBV made her dying much easier. "She kept saying, 'Denise.'" The daughter had no idea who Denise was. Then the mother said, "I have to go," and when asked where she had to go, said, "You just don't understand." Undeterred, the daughter says this happened a few times, and the family would just lay her back down and "...she would then again stare at the same spot up by the ceiling." The family told her it was okay to die, and the next day, an hour and a half after the family arrived, "...she simply winced, and then whispered what appeared to be the words, 'Love ya.'"

The daughter writes about how peaceful it was to watch her pass, how happy she was that her mother waited to die until after she got back from vacation. "Funny how things happen, huh? I'm not afraid to die now." [20]

21. SO HAPPY THAT WE EXPERIENCED IT WITH HER

A daughter writes, "I am sure my mom was having visions of someone, something, or maybe more than one." The mother would fix her eyes on a corner of the room and be totally intent on whatever she was watching, then turn her head as if following an object. Wills-Brandon calls this "The Stare," and says it happens quite often in dying patients.

Finally, "I am convinced it was something very spiritual, and I am so happy she experienced it and that we (my husband, son and I) experienced it with her." [21]

DISCUSSION

DBVs and their cousins, NDEs, have a long and cross-cultural history. They were artificially triggered with drugs and plants and used in initiation rituals in Native American cultures, ancient Egypt, and in African tribal rituals as late as the 20th century. Masonic initiation and even contemporary fraternity "hazing" probably have their roots in the practice of ritual triggering of NDEs and DBVs in order to help initiates lose their fear of death, which is closely related to achieving emotional maturity, and binds participants to one another in close relationships.

The most systematic modern research on DBVs has been done by Osis and Haraldsson and is described in their book, *At the Hour of Death*. They sent out 5700 questionnaires to doctors and nurses in India and the U.S. 1704 were returned, and 877 chosen for detailed follow-up interviews. Osis and Haraldsson believe that the results are strongly suggestive of life after death, but they do not claim to offer "proof."

Some of the details of their findings are remarkable. For instance, they found that a few patients had diseases known to cause hallucinations: anoxia, fever, mental illness, kidney disease, brain injury, hemorrhage and bleeding. Yet hundreds of the patients who had DBVs did not have these diseases, so it cannot be said that the visions are caused by the diseases.

Osis and Haraldsson also thought that if drugs were causing the visions, those patients taking drugs would have more visions. This also did not happen. Only 20% of the patients who were reported to have DBVs were receiving drugs, and those receiving drugs known to cause hallucinations did not have any more visions than those receiving no drugs. Osis and Haraldsson believe that something besides drugs and disease caused the DBVs.

The authors found another surprising fact: while visions in healthy people are 70% of the time focused on this-worldly situations, the great majority of visions in the dying focus on other-worldly situations. This might lead us to think that fear or emotional problems might be causing the visions.

Osis and Haraldsson found that fear and emotional problems also were not likely to cause the visions. Why do they conclude this? When asked whom they expected to see in the hospital on the day before their visions, almost no patients saw in their visions the people they expected to see, or even those people who had actually visited. Also, we might expect that patients who expected to die might be more likely to see visions of people who had predeceased them and that those who did not expect to die might see visions of living people and this-worldly environments. This simply did not happen. The authors found that apparitions of deceased loved ones and religious figures had agendas of their own, often contradicting the wishes or expectations of the patients.

From this, the authors concluded that the visions do not represent fear, or wish fulfillment, or expectations of the patients, but rather represent some force **external** to the patients.

But perhaps cultural, religious, and educational factors might influence the content of the visions. On this, Osis and Haraldsson have a great deal to say. In summary, they found that Americans with a Christian background did not usually meet the devil, or see the fires of hell, nor were they whisked off or dematerialized by the Grim Reaper. Hindus did not mention key Hindu ideas of reincarnation or dissolving back into the Higher Being at death. Instead, Christians saw God or Christ, Mary or angels, and Hindus saw Shiva, Krishna, Rama or Yama, the Hindu god of death, or messengers of Yama. Once again, most patients were surprised at the contents of their visions.

In another startling discovery, Osis and Haraldsson found that DBVs cut as cleanly across educational, cultural and gender differences as they cut across religious factors. The *experiences* dying patients have are almost identical across all these differences, but patients will *label* their experiences according to their religious tradition. Another way of saying this is that DBVs are core human experiences, and that religious and cultural beliefs grow together around these core experiences.

Melvin Morse in *Transformed by the Light* and in *Parting Visions* lists some ways in which the DBV and NDE are helpful to both patients and families. They validate the patients' own psychical awareness and help restore control and dignity to the death experience. Patients receive an impression of death quite different from the prevailing cultural attitude about death. Death is seen, about 90% of the time, as spiritual and wonderful, rather than frightening and painful people by who have or witness, DBVs. Visitors, and even medical personnel can become much less afraid of dying by being with patients who are having DBVs. Finally, it is encouraging to know that family members who know about DBVs and NDEs have been found to spend more time at the bedside of their loved ones. So not only is fear of death reduced for all concerned, but patients are less likely to feel isolated as they face their evident transition to another level of existence.

Taken together, the findings that DBVs are not apparently triggered by physical diseases, or drugs, or fear, or cultural or religious or gender or educational factors, and that the "helpers" who come to ease the transition often surprise the patients with an agenda of their own, leave us with a large question. Then what does trigger them? It seems reasonable to believe that they are triggered by something outside of the patient, and that something may well be a communication from people who have predeceased them, persons perceived as religious figures, or landscapes on another level of existence.

For all these reasons, Osis and Haraldsson, as well as Morse and Wills-Brandon, believe that there is strong evidence for a continuing life after the death of the body.

FOOTNOTES

1. From James Hyslop, cited by Ian Currie, *You Cannot Die,* Somerville House, Toronto, 1998, page 182.
2. *Ibid.,* page 183.
3. From William Barrett, cited by Currie, *Ibid.,* pages 11-12.
4. Melvin Morse and Paul Perry, *Parting Visions,* Judy Piatkus Publishing, Ltd., London, pages 51-55.
5. *Ibid.,* pages 56-57.
6. Karlis Osis and Erlendur Haraldsson, *At the Hour Of Death,* Avon Books, New York, 1977, page 35.
7. *Ibid.,* page38.
8. Carla Wills-Brandon, *One Last Hug Before I Go,* Health Communications, Deerfield Beach, FL, 2000, pages 77-78.
9. Osis and Haraldsson, *Op.Cit.,* page 40.
10. Cited by Wills-Brandon, *Op.Cit.,* page 219.
11. Osis and Haraldsson, *Op.Cit.,* pages 162-163.
12. *Ibid.,* page 164.
13. Ibid. page 164.
14. *Ibid.,* pages 165-166.
15. *Ibid.,* page 167.
16. *Ibid.,* page 126.
17. *Ibid.,* page 127.
18. *Ibid.,* page 127-128.
19. Wills-Brandon, *Op.Cit.,* pages 96-97.
20. *Ibid.,* page 8.

What if, in your dream,
you went to heaven
and there plucked
a strange and
beautiful flower?

And what if,
when you awoke,
you had the flower
in your hand?
Ah, what then?

-Samuel Taylor Coleridge

CHAPTER FIVE

OUT-OF-BODY EXPERIENCES

"What if you slept? And what if, in your sleep,
you dreamed? And what if, in your dream, you
went to heaven and there plucked a strange and
beautiful flower? And what if, when you awoke,
you had the flower in your hand? Ah, what then?"

Samuel Taylor Coleridge
(1772-1834)

The Out of Body Experience is one in which the subject feels that his or her consciousness is existing outside of the physical body. Almost always, people who have had an OBE are not only astonished, but are convinced that there is life beyond the death of the body. Skeptics point out that some drugs trigger OBEs, and that OBEs might be nothing but dreams, or psychological defenses against fear, and feel it is unlikely that anything actually leaves the body.

Out of Body Experiences are not so unusual. In a properly designed survey at the University of Virginia at Charlottesville, 25% of college students and 14% of townspeople reported that they had had an OBE. In another survey, Haraldsson reported that 8% of people in Iceland reported an OBE.[1]

And OBEs apparently happen in all cultures, to people of all religious traditions, and at all times in history. Some occur in Near Death Experiences, but in this chapter we will list cases in which the subject was not near death, but apparently healthy. Also, some OBEs are self-induced for experimental reasons.

FOUR LEVELS OF EVIDENCE

Currie [2] has suggested that OBEs can be divided into four levels of evidence as to whether "something" actually leaves the body during an OBE. The first level is convincing to the subject but usually not to others. The last three levels become more and more convincing to people who study them carefully and see them as part of a broad spectrum of psychic experiences.

LEVEL 1. Those in which the subject is alone and remains near the physical body.

LEVEL 2. Those in which the subject sees events or situations that she was not in a position to see, but that are later confirmed by others.

LEVEL 3. Those in which the subject projects himself to a distant place and is seen in apparitional form by someone in that place.

LEVEL 4. Those in which the subject is not only seen at a distant place by others but also accomplishes something there, such as touching, speaking, or carrying on a conversation.

LEVEL 1

1. RELIEF AND CURIOSITY

A chemistry professor at a major university recalls an experience he had, several times, as a student. While studying, he says, "My hands and work stayed down, but my view of my hands and work shifted to somewhere on the ceiling." He does not remember seeing the back of his head or the rest of his body, as in some OBE reports. And it was different from a dream, he says, in that dreams have an abrupt beginning and ending, but this experience seemed to be "a gradual lifting from the normal state." He was also afraid: "I couldn't find the mechanism of control, and wondered how I would get back." He forced himself to relax, not to panic, and soon found himself back at his desk. He reports not only relief, but also curiosity, and wondering if this kind of experience is something he could learn to do at will. He says that he does not remember any subsequent experiences of this type as he grew older, or whether he knew anything about OBEs before his student experience. He also does not remember whether he was overly tired.

2. THIS CANNOT BE A DREAM

A Mr. Huntley writes that he awoke from sleep to find himself outside of his body. The report is rather eloquent in that he says that he was conscious in two places – in a "feeble degree" in his body, and in "a great degree" away from the body. (It sounds as though he were literally beside himself.) "I was surrounded by a white opaque light," he reports, and says that he was absolutely happy and secure. He was also very observant: he thought that this could not have been a dream because his consciousness "...was an enhanced one as superior to the ordinary waking state as that is to the dream state." The experience was also vivid, so much so that he saw a thread between the two bodies, but said he believed that if that feeble thread between body and soul had been snapped, he himself would have remained intact.[3]

3. GOING TO THE DENTIST

In a dentist's chair and undergoing anesthesia, a patient had the sensation of waking and finding himself floating near the ceiling, watching the dentist at work on his body. He must have thought, "This is a bad dream," but then on another occasion, he was in a hotel and woke not feeling well. This time he fainted, and again says that he was near the ceiling observing his body. When he tried unsuccessfully to reenter the body, he says that he decided that he had died. He doesn't say that he was frightened, but his conclusion was mistaken, since he was also certain that he did not lose either memory or consciousness, and that he could see his own body "...like a separate object." He felt "immobilized," and when he heard a knock on the door, was not able to respond. Then he saw a hotel employee on the fire escape, a doctor was called in, and the subject says that he saw the doctor shake his head after listening to his heart. After all that, he must have been astounded when he woke up in bed.[4]

4. EXQUISITE BEYOND WORDS

Oliver Fox thought he was having a dream, but noticed that the stones on his sidewalk were not in their usual place. Then the quality of the dream changed. "Instantly," he says, "...the vividness of life increased, and never had the sky and sea and trees shone with such beauty." Then he said, "Never had I felt so absolutely well, so clear-brained, so divinely powerful, so inexpressibly free!" As though he had a loosened spirit, he says the feeling was "...exquisite beyond words, but it lasted only a few moments, and I awoke..." [5]

5. I FELT THE HAPPINESS GO THROUGH ME

A creative teacher, Samuel Silverstein, asked his children to draw pictures showing any strange feelings or experiences they had had. Careful not to suggest ideas to them, he says that D.E. brought a drawing to his desk and said, "This is what I saw happen to me Sunday in church." D.E. said that after saying a prayer she felt "sort of light" and then saw herself float up to the ceiling. Then a red line came from the sky, circling down, and headed toward her. The line came in near the shoulder, then went to her heart, but when it reached the heart, D.E. said, it turned to a yellow glow, and "red wiggly lines" started to spread out inside her body, filling it almost full. The yellow glow filled her whole body, and, D.E. said, a feeling of great happiness swept through her. In telling her story, this eight-year-old then paused with a look of peaceful joy on her face. Then, she said, there was "...a wind of some sort...like air rushing out..." And with some melancholy, "Well, the happy feeling lasted a long time.... And the feeling of something inside of me pushing out was gone...and the happiness was gone too." [6]

6. THE DOG WAS CONFUSED

A doctor writes that he seemed to "step out" of his body, stood beside it, and looked down on it. Feeling light as air, he thought, "This must be what St. Paul calls the Spiritual Body." He moved toward the door, and was surprised to find that he simply passed through it. "I knew," he said, "that a cold wind was blowing... but I was not chilled." He must have been quite curious, because he went back into the room to get another look at his body. While there, he noticed that his dog Leo had awakened. The dog approached the physical body, wagged his tail sniffed at his legs, then appeared confused. His master was utterly in evidence in two places! He sniffed again, sat down and looked up, and "...uttered a mournful howl." The doctor is expressive, saying that Leo apparently saw him standing at the door, and with a single leap, "took his place between me and the body..." He looked first at one, then at the other, and "...trembled in evident agony." [7]

7. PERFECTLY HAPPY ABOUT DYING

A pastor, Reverend O.A. Ostby woke from sleep one night, as he said, "in clear full consciousness." He must have been dumbfounded to see himself standing by his bed looking at his physical body. "I knew at once that I, my real self, was outside of my body and that I had passed through what is called Death." He claims, perhaps unbelievably, that he was "perfectly happy" about dying, but concerned about the shock to his wife and baby son. So he decided to "...try to reanimate..." his physical body again. Then he felt himself lifted from the floor, "laid horizontally in space, and pushed slowly, inch by inch, into the physical again." He could tell, he says, "...when my heart started to beat again and the blood to circulate through my veins." This slow re-entry is unusual – more often it is described as a shock or a jolt.[8]

LEVEL 2

Level 2 cases are those in which the projector notices something that her physical body was in no position to observe, and the accuracy of the observation is confirmed by others.

8. LOS ANGELES TO OMAHA

This case is a combination of levels 2 and 3. Mr. Cronk, living in Los Angeles, was fortunate to be taking a Saturday afternoon nap, when he found himself in Omaha at his parents' home. He says that the experience was "... more real than a dream." In very ordinary language, he reports that he saw his mother sitting on a sofa, and lay down and put his head on her lap. After some time, he heard his wife (in Los Angeles) calling him and immediately found himself back in his physical body in Los Angeles. He described a number of things he had observed in his parents' house, including the dress which his mother was wearing.

On the following Monday, he must have been surprised to receive an airmail letter from his mother, saying that she had seen her son enter her room at about 2:00 p.m. his time, which would have been 12:00 her time. In later letters she confirmed her son's observations of how she was dressed, how the furniture was arranged, and so on.[9]

9. NEW YORK TO ICELAND

This well-known case is one of the most staggering of all of the examples of OBEs. It involves Mrs. Eileen Garrett, one of the great mediums of the 20th Century, who worked for many years with the American Society for Psychical Research. Coordinating with Dr. Anita Muhl in New York and Dr. D. Svenson in Reykyavik, Iceland, Mrs. Garrett was supposed to visit, out of her body, Dr. Svenson, where he had set up certain experimental conditions.

In her projected state, Mrs. Garrett says that she sensed the humid atmosphere, and saw and smelled flowers that were growing in a garden, then passed through walls to a room where the experiment was to take place. No one was there, she saw, but at that moment Dr. Svenson walked down the stairs and like a good researcher said, "This will be a successful experiment." Then he instructed her to look at the objects on the table and to describe them aloud to the secretary in New York who was taking notes. She heard Dr. Svenson say, "Make my apologies to the experimenters at your end. I have had an accident and cannot work as well as I had hoped." She could see that his head was bandaged and described the bandage. Apparently in both places at the same time, she overheard Dr. Muhl in New York say, "This can't possibly be true. I had a letter a few days ago and the doctor was quite well then." Then Dr. Svenson walked to his bookcase, and Mrs. Garrett knew what book he was thinking of and its position on the shelf. He opened it and held the title up as if to show her, and Mrs. Garrett read the title and gave a sense of the paragraph in her own words.

The results were sent by mail to Dr. Svenson, and the next morning Dr. Muhl received a telegram, reporting that Dr. Svenson had suffered an accident just before the experiment that caused his head to be bandaged. The other details were sent by mail, and proved to be accurate in each detail.[10]

10. SOMEONE IS LYING

As an adult, a man in Sweden remembers an event that happened when he was five years old. He had a throat ailment, and a decision was made to operate. Naturally afraid, as most children would be, his mother had told him that "definitely" Dr. Widen would be the surgeon, and since Dr. Widen was an acquaintance of the family, this was reassuring to the patient. "Suddenly," he says, "I saw the room in a wonderful light without shadows." His hands had been tied with straps, but when he tried to move them, he found that "...they were dead." Then, he says, "Astonished, I slid down onto the floor and looked at myself." Then he saw a "...young, dark-haired doctor..." and a white box with instruments, which frightened him. When he woke up, he told his mother that he had not seen Dr. Widen during the surgery, but his mother said, "How do you know? After all you were asleep." But when the doctors made their rounds, this brave five-year old complained again. A doctor said, "What could you know about that? You were asleep." The boy replied, "No, I stood to one side and watched." Afterward, he says, the nurses "bawled me out," saying, "...you don't talk to doctors that way. Doctors are gods." Indeed! The records show that the surgery was performed by another doctor, Dr. A.M.., though Dr. Widen was in the clinic at the time. This was a poor trick to play on a five year old.[11]

11. A COIL OF LIGHT...LIKE A GARDEN HOSE

One especially clear description of an OBE is by the British writer, William Gerhardi in his book, *Resurrection*. He says he had gone to bed exhausted and dreamed of pulling a broken tooth from his mouth. He woke, he thought, and reached to press a light switch above his head, but could not and said he was "...grasping the void." He found himself floating, and said the room was all darkness, but all around him was a "milky, pellucid light, like steam." At one point he looked behind him and saw "a coil of light...like a garden hose," which extended back to his physical body sleeping on the bed. Trying to open the door, he "...had no grip," so went through the door into the bathroom where he saw his second body in a mirror. He wandered the house, then felt himself fly out through the front door and snap back into his sleeping physical body.

As he became more skilled, there were other projections, in which he observed distant events and had them confirmed. This included proof from another person who had seen him while he was out of body, and a visit to strangers after which he accurately described them to someone who knew them. His most striking report is that he met, during an out of body excursion, the spirit of a friend named Bonzo. Together they decided to visit Bonzo's house, where they found Bonzo's physical body, dead. In the morning, Gerhardi called Bonzo's home and learned that he had in fact died the day before, during surgery for a broken wrist. This sounds doubtful, but even in modern medicine people sometimes react dangerously and fatally to anesthesia. Gerhardi reports that he had not known of the injury.[12]

12. BEING OUT OF THE BODY <u>VS</u>. SEEING AT A DISTANCE

One of the important questions about OBEs is whether in some sense the person projecting is "really there" at the place he claims to have projected, or whether he is getting a telepathic or clairvoyant message about the target, perhaps "plucked" from the mind of the experimenter.

Dr. Osis, at the ASPR, devised an experiment to discover which of these processes was happening. This experiment has become a classic in psychical research. A shelf, divided by a partition, had two trays, one on either side of the partition. In the trays were the target materials. The shelf was suspended from the ceiling, two feet below it, out of view of the persons who was supposed to project. Because of the partition and the ceiling, only the materials on one side could be seen from that side of the shelf, and only the materials on the other side, from the other side of the shelf. A clever researcher, Dr. Osis thought that if his subject was seeing clairvoyantly, he could see all the objects, but if he was actually projecting, he would see only the objects on the tray nearest him.

The projector, an artist named Ingo Swann, was seated on a chair below the shelf, where all objects there were out of his vision, and was connected by cables to a polygraph in the next room.

Mr. Swann was instructed to "go" to certain locations around the shelf, and to sketch what he had seen. The objects in the trays were strong shapes, such as an umbrella, a cross, a black leather case, a red heart with a black dagger across it, a bull's eye within three circles. Swann sketched the objects almost exactly, from different vantage points to which he had been instructed to go. He correctly sketched the bull's eye, but with the colors wrong, a large red circle, a quarter moon, and round geometric figures that looked like dumplings he called "round dumpy things."

In a refinement of this experiment, objects were placed in a closed box with a small opening, like a birdhouse, and the objects could be seen only when viewed through a mirror. Swann's drawings showed that he saw the objects in reverse, as one does through a mirror.

The results were evaluated by a psychologist who correctly matched Swann's drawings with the objects that could be seen from the various positions. Statistically, according to Osis, there was one chance in 40,000 of achieving Swann's results.[13]

13. CHARLES TART AND MISS Z.

Another experiment was done by Charles Tart, Ph.D., of the University of

California, a well-known researcher on OBEs. He worked with a remarkable young woman, Miss Z., who claimed she had had OBEs since childhood, and thought everyone had them. Tart spent four nights in the laboratory with Miss Z., who was in bed with electrodes attached to her head. Any movement out of the bed would have triggered huge signals in the EEG machine. When she was ready to go to sleep, Tart would go into another room, open a book of random numbers, randomly select a five-digit sequence, write it on a piece of paper, slip it into a folder, and the slip the folder onto a shelf well above Miss Z's head. He would remind her that the number was there and that she should read and memorize the number if her OBE took her to that vicinity, and she was to note the time on the clock which was also on the shelf.

On three of the nights, Miss Z. said that she was not in a position to see the numbers. But on one night, she said she saw the number and reported it to be 25132. This was correct, and Tart calculated the odds of correctly guessing a five-digit number (only one guess) are 100,000 to 1.[14]

14. CARL JUNG VISITS HIS NEIGHBOR

In *Memories, Dreams, Reflections* Jung tells of an experience of his own. He was lying awake thinking of a friend and neighbor whose funeral had taken place on the day before. Suddenly it seemed that the friend was at the foot of Jung's bed, asking Jung to go somewhere with him. Jung thought, like a trained psychologist, that it was an inner fantasy, but then asked himself, "Do I have any proof that this is a fantasy?" Jung decided that if it were not a fantasy, then it would be "abominable" of him to ignore his friend, and that he should give the friend the benefit of the doubt and "credit him with reality." Abominable may seem a strong word, but it did motivate Dr. Jung to take action.

The friend led him out of the house, into the garden, out to the road, and finally to the friend's house. He conducted Jung to the study, and there he climbed on a stool and showed Jung the second of five books with red bindings, which stood on the second shelf from the top. Apparently the shelves were high, as Jung could not see the titles, only the red color.

Jung was of course curious, so on the next day he went to the friend's house and asked if he could look up something in his friend's library. Not surprisingly, there was the stool, and Jung could see the five books with red bindings. But he must have been astonished when he stepped up on the stool and read the title of the second volume; it was *The Legacy of the Dead*. Jung says that he was not acquainted with the friend's library, and did not know what books he owned, so his knowledge of the location and title of the book, with its possible connection to the death of his friend, are very strange indeed. [15]

LEVEL 3

Level 3 cases are those in which the projector is seen at the location to which she has projected. More than the previous ones, these cases stretch our imaginations, and are more difficult to believe. Clear thinking is especially important on these cases, as all of us have prejudices which we do not normally recognize.

We have pointed out earlier a very important fact that scientists can forget: F.C.S Schiller emphasizes that "Single facts can never be 'proved' except by their coherence in a system. But, as all facts come singly, anyone who dismisses them one by one is destroying the conditions under which a conviction of new truth could arise in his mind."[16] In other words, these reports sound quite incredible if we view them singly. But as part of a "system" to which Schiller refers, they seem more credible and help us to a deeper understanding of the truth.

15. A CREATIVE WAY TO GO TO CHURCH

A pastor, W.T. Stead, tells a story of a woman who was a member of his church, but was lying home one Sunday with a fever. Presumably, very few pastors have such stories to tell. During the evening service, her solid figure entered the church, walked up the aisle in full view of everyone present, and sat down. She picked up a hymn book, but did not sing, and an usher offered her another hymnal. She did not contribute to the collection box. Following the last hymn, she stood up, still holding the book, laid it down and walked quickly down the aisle, opened the door, and left. According to the pastor, she was seen by him, and by several others, and had sat in the pew she normally occupied.

On further checking, the woman told Stead that she had had a strong wish to go to church, but knew she was too sick to go. After receiving medicine from a doctor, she slept during the period of the service, not knowing that her second body was seen in church.

This case is unusually well documented. Stead was a reasonable and experienced investigator, and four other people saw her who were acquainted with her. These witnesses and the doctor all signed statements, as well as the members of her family who were at home with her while she was projecting.[17]

16. A MELANCHOLY STORY FROM FRANCE

The French astronomer-psychic researcher, Flammarion, reports another church case. A young pastor was delivering a sermon while his fiancee was lying extremely ill at her home, though apparently he was not aware of the seriousness of her condition. She went into a trance during the service, and

A melancholy Story from France

woke two hours later, saying that she had been in church and heard his sermon. Shortly afterward, she died. There must have been great sadness as well as great astonishment, because after the funeral, the girl's mother asked the pastor what he had said in the sermon, and it matched perfectly what the girl had told her mother. And there was more: the pastor added, "It is very strange, but in the middle of my sermon, I thought I saw a white figure enter the church, resembling my fiancee." He reported that she had sat down, but disappeared near the end of the service.[18]

17. FARMER MCBRIDE'S FATHER

An Indiana bachelor farmer had gone to bed, according to his normal routine, when suddenly "…preposterous as it sounds…" he found himself floating. He was wide awake, and floating through the ceiling and upper floor of the house, unintentionally flying north, toward his old home where his father was still living. He passed through walls and entered his father's bedroom, where he stood at the foot of the bed and saw his father lying there. The son said, "Father, Father!" and says that his father was watching him with a look of surprise. Having been concerned about his father during the day, and thinking he might be ill, he was relieved to see that his father was well.

Apparently not one to linger, the younger McBride left and found himself back in his own bedroom, where he says "…I saw… my own body, still lying on the bed where I had left it…" He wrote down what had happened, then two days later, on Christmas Day, he visited his father. The elder McBride had two visitors at the same time, and witnessed to them that he had seen his son, two days earlier, standing at the foot of his bed, and had written down the time. The time was correct.[19]

18. ALL THE WAY TO KENYA

A Mr. Herbert reports that one time, while he was living in England, he projected to the home of a friend then living in Kenya. He was unfamiliar with the house, having never seen it, and while he was there, was visible to the friend's two young daughters.

While he was projected there he could see "…the house and everything about it…" While the two little girls were looking at him, their mother called and asked what they were doing. "Looking at Nunkie" was their reply. "And they certainly were," says Herbert. "They were looking right at me." They seemed confused about how he got there. Later, when he wrote his friends he described the house and how he had seen the two children. The friends wrote back saying that his description of the arrangement of the rooms, the windows, etc. was very accurate. They included a photo of an unusual window which he had correctly described.[20]

19. A TEACHER WITH MANY SKILLS

Even though there were fifty witnesses to this story, it remains one of the most difficult to accept.

Mlle Sage

In France, thirty-two year old Emile Sagee taught at an exclusive school for girls, the Pensionnat de Neuwelcke. She was well liked by students and by the directors of her school, and was said to be an excellent teacher.

But the students began to notice something remarkable about their teacher: there were sometimes two of her. Initially, their comments to the school administrators were dismissed as childish imagination, but when thirteen students in one class saw two identical teachers in the front of the room, the administrators became concerned. Could this be a group hallucination, or was something even stranger happening? As Ms. Sagee was writing on the blackboard, an identical figure appeared beside her and wrote with the same motions. Later, a student standing with her teacher looked into a mirror and saw two Ms. Sagees. The student fainted. (Probably sufficient cause for a lawsuit.)

As time passed, Ms. Sagee was seen not only by students, but by serving employees in the dining room. Once while Ms. Sagee was eating, another Ms. Sagee appeared behind her making the same motions. Also, the two figures began to appear at greater distances from one another: one day forty two students were playing in a large room while Ms. Sagee sat in an armchair watching. When one of the students looked out the window, she saw Ms. Sagee picking flowers outside in the garden. According to the story, the figure in the garden initially appeared as if in a trance, but then when the figure on the chair disappeared, the garden figure became more animated. This kind of event happened several times, with one figure seeming as if in a trance, and the weaker the trance-like figure appeared, the more solid would be the appearance of the second figure. It was as though the two figures borrowed energy from a common source.

Confronted, Ms. Sagee claimed not to know these events were occurring, but with pressure from parents and administrators, she was reluctantly dismissed. Later it came out that she had been relieved of duty for the same reason, of being seen double, in previous schools.

With fraudulent stories, there will usually be some benefit to the reported projector, such as money or status. In this case, the projecting brought nothing but trouble for Ms. Sagee, so we have to wonder if indeed the story has truth in it. Also, Ms. Sagee may not have been in control of the events. This bi-location would be a serious handicap in her retaining a job, if the stories are true.[21]

20. AN OVER-RESPONSIBLE EMPLOYEE
R.P. Roberts, an apprentice in a dry-goods shop, had a schedule of going

home for lunch at noon each day and returning at twelve-thirty. One day, eating his meal, he looked at the clock and saw that it said twelve-thirty. He was alarmed, thinking that he would be late returning, but when he looked again at the clock it said twelve-fifteen.

At twelve-fifteen back at the shop, his employer, Mrs. Owen, saw him enter the shop, go behind the counter and hang up his hat. She rather rudely remarked to her husband and a customer that her employee had come at a time when he was not needed. After she said this, he took his hat and left the shop, and Mrs. Owen said that he looked "quite absent-minded and vague." Perhaps he had been insulted!

When the apprentice returned again at twelve-thirty, Mrs. Owen asked him to explain his strange behavior. He told her that he was at home at twelve-fifteen, but the other three people insisted that he had been in the shop at that time. To make things more complicated, Roberts' aunt, who had eaten lunch with him, swore that he had been at home at twelve-fifteen, that he did not leave the table until about twelve twenty-five, when he left for the shop.

Later, Roberts reported that at twelve-fifteen, he had a strong sense that he should be at the shop, and Mrs. Owen reported that at twelve-fifteen a customer had come in wanting an article that only Roberts could have found. (Does a strong sense of responsibility trigger OBEs?)[22]

LEVEL 4

Level 4 cases are those in which the projector actually does something at the location where she is sighted. In regard to astonishing cases like these, F.W.H. Myers believed, like Schiller, that scientific caution and humility are not enough. He also thought that "A certain boldness is required, a readiness to grasp a vast range of converging evidence, each of which, standing alone, can lead us nowhere." [23]

21. YOU ARE THE ONE WHO CAME TO CHEER ME UP

Ms. Katheryn Riggs wrote a letter describing an event that happened when she was a surgery patient, some years before. She relates how another patient was brought into the ward, and placed some distance from Ms. Riggs. Apparently the woman was in considerable pain, and Ms. Riggs says that "Her moans were pitiful" and during the night, she said, "… I felt I wanted to go to her and say something to comfort her." With extraordinary compassion, she felt herself leave her body and went down the ward to the other patient. "I spoke to her for a little while, and then I said, 'I must leave you now or my body will be cold.'" She returned to her bed and saw her own body lying on it. Later, she told the sister about it and the sister was very interested, saying that she would take Ms. Riggs to the other patient when she was able to go. When she went, the other woman said, "Oh...I know you...you are the one who came in here to cheer me up...when I was so ill." [24]

22. PADRE PIO AND GENERAL LUIGI CADORNA

There are a number of well-documented reports and even a television show about bi-locations of Padre Pio, a 20th Century Italian Capuchin monk. General Cadorna was a commander of the Italian Army in World War I. He had suffered a number of defeats and was severely depressed. He decided to commit suicide, and ordered the guard to let no one into his tent. The report is dramatic: while he held a pistol to his head, he saw a monk enter, who looked at him for a moment and said, "Such an action is foolish." Then the vision left as abruptly as it had come. The commander says that he put down his gun and wondered who this strange monk could have been. General Cadorna had never seen Padre Pio, but after the war he heard about the priest and decided to pay him a visit. When he saw the monk, he recognized him as the one who had visited him in the tent. [25]

23. MRS. WILMOT AND THE MERCHANT MARINE

This case is very well documented and happened at sea when the ship Mr. Wilmot was aboard encountered a storm on the way from Liverpool to New York. Mr. Wilmot says that he dreamed that he saw his wife come to the door of his stateroom, clad only in her night-dress. She modestly hesitated at the door when she saw that he was not alone, then entered, stooped down, and kissed him, then quietly withdrew. When he woke, he said, he saw his fellow-passenger whose berth was above his, leaning on his elbow and teasing, "You're a pretty fellow, to have a lady come and visit you in this way."

Naturally, Wilmot questioned his bunkmate at length, and his description of Mrs. Wilmot's visit matched exactly with Mr. Wilmot's experience in the dream. This may not have been a dream, since, when he met his wife in Watertown, Connecticut, she asked, "Did you receive a visit from me a week ago Tuesday?" Mr. Wilmot doubted that it was more than a coincidence, but she told him that she was concerned because of the severity of the weather, and went out to look for him. In fact, she asked if the ship had upper berths that extended out further than the lower ones, since that is what she saw. This was a precise description of the state-room, which was at the rear of the vessel and was constructed in that way. She also said that a man was in the upper berth, looking at her, and for that reason she (modestly) hesitated to go in. Mrs. Wilmot not only apparently traveled, but was seen, gave an accurate description of the place where she projected, and took action by kissing her husband before she withdrew. [26]

THINKING CRITICALLY ABOUT THE OBE

Of course, the central question concerning OBEs is, does "something" really go out of the body? The answer is important for the question of life after death. If "something" goes out of the body before death, then perhaps that same "something" can survive after the death of the body.

We know that virtually every major spiritual tradition assumes the survival of a soul, and that people who have OBEs are usually convinced not only that a "spirit" or "spiritual body" really goes out of the physical body, but are also convinced about life after death.

But we also know that some dreams are very much like OBEs, that certain psychological problems trigger OBEs, and some drugs, both legal and illegal, seem related to OBEs.

DREAMS?

Concerning dreams, most skeptics who believe OBEs are nothing but dreams point out that dreams often involve peculiar body sensations, vibrations, noises, flying, rising out of the body, etc. So we can believe that some OBEs, particularly Level 1 type events, may be dream related. But this theory does not come close to explaining OBEs in Levels 2, 3, 4.

PSYCHOLOGICAL PROBLEMS?

On the other hand, skeptics trained in psychology often believe that what appears as an OBE is actually a product of fear, self-centeredness, wishful thinking, pathological hallucination, or some other altered state of consciousness. Again, it is possible that some Level 1 OBEs could fit into this theory. But to try to explain Levels 2, 3, and 4 in this way leads to strange and complicated speculations. For example, some have tried to explain Level 3 OBEs as collective hallucinations, in which one person claiming to have seen the OBE projector "infects" others who then have the same hallucination. Yet there is no evidence that mental patients, or healthy people, "catch" hallucinations by infection.

DRUGS, ANOXIA, PHYSICAL CHANGES?

Finally, some claim that OBEs are nothing but reactions to drugs, notably ketamine or LSD, or reactions to brain changes during the death process. Yet, except for cases 3, 10 and 16, the case studies in this chapter are chosen because they did not happen to people who were ill or dying, but to healthy people, who were not using or being treated with drugs. Of course it is possible for the person reporting a case to leave out an important detail regarding drugs, but this is no explanation for the large number of cases in Levels 2, 3, and 4, and the hundreds of cases not included in this chapter. Finally, drugs have not been shown to trigger NDEs, or DBVs, as we explored at some length in Chapter Two. And drugs certainly do not explain the higher level OBEs, in which accurate information is gathered by the projector, or the projector is seen or does something at the place of projection. It seems unlikely that anyone would try to explain these kinds of events as drug-related.

MILITANT SKEPTICISM?

But there are other skeptical people, perhaps those who have an emotional commitment to their skepticism, who make different arguments.

Some militant skeptics react to this material by refusing to accept the existence of the evidence for the OBE being what it appears to be. Here is an example: these skeptics sometimes say that many of these reported events happened either a long time ago, or are from surveys or anecdotes. Even worse, they say, they are legends or myths that grew up around peculiar events, or are things that happen only to the feeble minded, the sick, the dying, or the ignorant, and probably fit into superstitions those people already held. As Carl Becker points out, as strong as these objections sound, they really are based on ignorance of the facts.[27]

The passage of time does not invalidate or validate these reports, but it in fact subjects them to intense scrutiny, and has led to discarding weak cases. Further, there is no evidence at all that these experiences happen **only** to the feeble-minded, the sick, the dying or the ignorant. Careful study by Walter Prince and Hornell Hart shows the responsibility, modern skeptical attitudes and calm states of mind of many of the perceivers. Also, there is wide agreement among OBE projectors about the nature of the events that happen, even though they have not communicated with each other. And most people who have OBEs had them before they were aware that such things happen. Finally, OBEs have even been experimentally produced and confirmed by independent testing agencies[28] Aware of the difficulty many people properly have in trusting such reports as those in this chapter, Hornell Hart rated 165 cases on a "scale of evidentiality" to test their consistency, clear-headedness, and tendency to report unsupported claims. When statistical checks were applied to see if "low evidentiality cases" showed an inclination toward being more wonderful, striking, or sensational, than the "high evidentiality cases," Hart's finding was conclusive: there is no difference.[29] So reports of more remarkable cases such as those in Levels 2, 3, and 4 are no less well documented than cases on Level 1. In fact, they really are better documented, since more than one witness was involved in the higher level cases.

PARAPSYCHOLOGY IN INTELLIGENCE AND DETECTIVE WORK

For security, intelligence, and parapsychology buffs, the issue of the use of psychical research in intelligence and detective work has endless fascination. Unfortunately, whatever is fascinating to the public becomes the victim of media hype and considerable spin. Since there are many books and Internet websites devoted to these subjects, we will give a brief summary only. The overlap with research on life after death is this: in out-of-body experience research, we have explored whether "something" actually goes out of the body during an OBE. If it does, then some assume that this "something" might also survive the death of the physical body.

In intelligence work, a more common term is "remote viewing" in which a psychic gains an impression of features of a distant location. The Russians call it "psychotronics." It is quite clear that such phenomena do occur. What is not clear, among other things, is whether "something" goes out of the body of the remote viewer to visit a site, or whether some image of a distant location somehow comes into the body of the viewer who is not remote. In view of this, some wish to distinguish OBEs from remote viewing.

There are a number of facts that seem quite well established. For decades, U.S., Russian and Chinese intelligence agencies were, and perhaps still are, involved in research on remote viewing and have attempted to view remotely each other's military secrets. Significant money has been spent, and significant conflict has been generated over this research. Because almost all of the material is classified, a sense of mystery has flourished. Claims of great success by some psychics and investigators are balanced by significant failures, so that "believers" and "unbelievers", even in the military establishment, have been arguing bitterly, and it has been difficult, especially in military and intelligence circles, to have objective, scientific assessments of psychic functioning.

Here are some selected highlights of this very large field. Parapsychology is not so far a proven intelligence tool. In 1971, laser physicist, Dr. Russell Targ of the Stanford Research Institute, met with CIA personnel. In 1972, an experiment was done at SRI in which a subject was startlingly accurate in describing out-of-sight objects, and the CIA encouraged the development of a more complete research plan. Numerous subjects were tested, including Alex Tanous, Ingo Swann, Pat Price, and results were sometimes astonishing, but at the same time spotty. The same psychic who produced impressive results on one day might produce nothing the next day. This of course raises the possibility of coincidence. Different subjects produced wildly different results: for instance, one subject could increase the temperature in an electronic machine, another could reproduce information inside sealed envelopes.

In one especially striking episode, SRI, working with two subjects, targeted a vacation property in the eastern United States. The geographic coordinates of the property were given the SRI physicists, who passed them on to the psychics. No maps were permitted, and the psychics were to describe what they viewed at that location. The psychics' descriptions were somewhat similar, but did not match the vacation property. Further investigation by the contact in the east discovered that there was in fact a sensitive government installation a few miles from the vacation property, which apparently the psychics had mistaken for the vacation property. On further questioning, they were able to give a list of project titles, the codename of the site, and accurate information about the layout of the site, but they gave incorrect names of people at the site.

According to Kenneth Kress,[30] at one time Project Officer for the Office of Technical Services, active funding for psychical research had, at the time of his writing, shifted to the Air Force's Foreign Technology Division. Apparently, the results of some simpler experiments have been very impressive and conclusive.

Ingo Swann, one of the psychics involved in the research, says in a 1995 article[31] that in fact remote viewers did help to find SCUD missiles, did help find biological and chemical warfare projects, and did locate tunnels and underground facilities, though he doesn't mention these locations, probably because they are overseas but classified.

For a time it appeared that research would be expanded, but events took a downturn. Personnel changes in the government and financial pressures caused serious disagreements on experimental procedures. One attempt at remote viewing of a Soviet installation by Pat Price produced mostly wrong data, when compared with fly-over photographs. Yet he accurately described buildings under construction, spherical tank sections, a crane, but there was so much bad information mixed with the good that it was not considered useful. The skeptical committee decided that the results were, when positive, no more than lucky guessing.

Overall, some results of the research for the Department of Defense defy explanation, coincidence is statistically unlikely, and fraud has not been discovered. Yet because of inconsistency of results, lack of a fundamental understanding of psychic events, and poor reproducibility, this research remains controversial and receives little official government support. Those who did work in the field are constrained by security requirements, and often do not stand up to report the positive aspects of the research. And just as important, they understandably do not want their reputations tarnished when the media distort even their correct descriptions of straightforward experimental work.

In 1961, Stephen I. Abrams of the Parapsychological Laboratory in London summarized the situation: for intelligence purposes Level II OBEs are demonstrated, but not understood or controllable. To this date, there seems to be little evidence of further development in this field.

SUBTOPIC: PSYCHIC DETECTIVES
While the media hype this topic for an eager public, it is notoriously difficult to find any responsible research on the effectiveness of psychic detective work. Individual psychics, such as Jean Dixon, claim spectacular successes, but we should expect some successes as a logical use of psychic abilities that we have described in these chapters. But authenticating reports in this field must rely on a case-by-case evaluation. Both psychic spy work and psychic detective work need better theoretical understanding, better control, and more concrete validation before we can place much reliance on their work.

The OBE has been studied far longer, and in greater depth, than the work of psychic spies or psychic detectives. More research in all three areas is likely to increase understanding. For the present the OBE seems well established and is claimed to be the most important strand of evidence for life after the death of the body.

FOOTNOTES

1. Susan Blackmore, *Beyond the Body,* Academy Chicago Publishers, Chicago, 1982, pages 85-87.
2. Ian Currie, *You Cannot Die,* Somerville House, Toronto, 1998, pages 115-122.
3. Robert Crookall, *The Study and Practice of Astral Projection,* Citadel Press, Secaucus, NJ, 1960, page 36.
4. Cited by Robert Almeder, *Death And Personal Survival,* Rowman and Littlefield, Publishers, Lanham, MD, 1992, page 165.
5. H.F.P. Battersby, *Man Outside Himself,* Citadel Press, Secaucus, NJ, 1969, page 77.
6. Susy Smith, *The Enigma of Out-Of Body Travel,* Helix Press, New York, 1965, pages 121-122.
7. Crookall, *Op. Cit.,* pages 38-39.
8. Battersby, *Op. Cit.,* page 40.
9. Robert Crookall, *Casebook of Astral Projection 545-746,* Citadel Press, Secaucus, NJ, 1980, page 48.
10. Smith, *Op. Cit.,* pages 72-74.
11. Nils Jacobson, *Life Without Death,* Dell Publishing, New York, 1974, pages 104-105.
12. Herbert Greenhouse, *The Astral Journey,* Avon Books, New York, 1974, pages 181-182.
13. *Ibid.,* pages 278-280.
14. Charles Tart, *Mind Body Spirit,* Hampton Roads Publishing Company, Charlottesville, VA, 1997, pages 178-179.
15. Smith, *Op. Cit.,* pages 154-155.
16. *Ibid.,* page 128.
17. Greenhouse, *Op. Cit.,* pages 78-79.
18. *Ibid.,* page 79.
19. Currie, *Op. Cit.,* pages 117-118.
20. *Ibid.,* pages 118-119.
21. Greenhouse, *Op. Cit.,* pages 84-87.
22. *Ibid.,* pages 83-84.
23. Smith, *Op. Cit.,* page 128.
24. Sylvan Muldoon and Hereward Carrington, *The Projection of the Astral Body,* Samuel Weiser, York Beach, ME, 1970, page 177.
25. Greenhouse, *Op. Cit.,* page 75.
26. Robert Crookall, *The Study and Practice of Astral Projection,* Citadel Press, Secaucus. NJ, 1960, pages 48-50.
27. Carl Becker, *Paranormal Experience and Survival of Death,* State University of New York Press, Albany, NY, 1993, pages 64-76.
28. Cited by Becker, *Ibid.,* pages 64-65.
29. Cited by Becker, *Ibid.,* page 65.
30. "Parapsychology In Intelligence: A Personal Review and Conclusions," by Dr. Kenneth A. Kress, at www.parascope.com/ds/articles/parapsychologyDoc.htm This report was released to the public in 1996.
31. "Ingo Swann on CIA/ESP Connection" at www.mindspring.com/~txporter/iswann.htm This does not seem to have been printed in a book or magazine.

KEY WORDS FOR INTERNET SEARCH

CIA PSYCHIC RESEARCH
PSYCHIC DETECTIVES
PSYCHIC SPIES
PARAPSYCHOLOGY IN INTELLIGENCE

CHAPTER SIX

APPARITIONS

"This rag-bag of assorted visions and
apparitions ...are more convincing because
honest investigators have done their best
to confirm that they are genuine. And
anyone who is willing to spend a few hours
browsing through volumes of the *Proceedings*
of the SPR (Society for Psychical Research....)
is bound to end with a feeling that further
skepticism is a waste of time. Even if half
the cases proved to be fraudulent or misreported,
the other half would still be overwhelming by
reason of sheer volume." [1]

In the chapter on Out-of Body Experiences, we saw evidence that inside the physical body lives another, different kind of body, often called the spiritual body. Even while the physical body is alive, this spiritual body can sometimes emerge as an out-of-body experience. But this spiritual body can also appear at the time of death of the physical body, or after death. Then it is called an apparition. Many people believe that apparitions are the strongest evidence we have of a life after the death of the body, and apparitions have been studied very carefully for over a century.

There are different kinds of apparitions, and these will be discussed by topic below. We will look at case reports of crisis apparitions, collectively perceived apparitions (seen by more than one person), apparitions of the dead, and haunting apparitions. Most of these cases were investigated and/or written up in the research literature on them. For this study, an apparition that appears in a dream is still considered an apparition because the issues of message and verifiability seem to be the same in either case.

CRISIS APPARITIONS

1. BERTIE

In this case from England, the writer tells that when he was fifteen years old, he spent some time at the home of a Dr. G, who had a cousin, age seventeen, named Bertie. The writer and Bertie became close friends, and one night Dr. G. was sent for to see Bertie, who had suddenly become ill with a lung inflammation. Bertie died the next night, but the writer had not been told of his condition, or his death. On the night following Bertie's death, the writer says that he was alone, reading, when Bertie walked in. Apparently Bertie looked real, and his gait did not suggest there was anything wrong with him.

Bertie

He did look cold and had no overcoat, and it was snowing, so the writer got up to get him a chair near the fire. Not suspecting anything unusual, the writer scolded him for coming out without a coat, but Bertie did not speak, and put his hand to his chest and shook his head. Except for being somewhat pale, Bertie appeared normal and walked across the room and sat near the fireplace while the writer continued talking, thinking that Bertie had lost his voice because of a cold. Then Dr. G. came in, and the writer told Dr. G. that Bertie had worn no coat, even in a snowstorm. After all this, the doctor informed him that Bertie had been dead for about half an hour. The apparition had been so lifelike that the writer had talked to Bertie for five minutes until Dr. G. had arrived. We don't know whether the apparition had forgotten his coat, or whether apparitions do not need coats! The writer must have felt deep sadness at the death of his friend, and complete astonishment as well.[2]

2. A DEATH PACT

In a case from France, two very close friends had promised each other that, if one died, she would make every effort to appear to the other, kiss her and say goodbye. The promise was kept, and some months later, one of the young women woke during the night and saw her friend. She heard the apparition tell her farewell, that she was dying. Though most of us would not fall asleep after such an event, this sleeper must have been very tired since she did go back to sleep, but an hour later felt her friend kiss her forehead. This last event happened at 4:00 in the morning. The second visit was more successful at waking the sleeper, and the living young woman inquired and learned at 5:00 that her friend had indeed died an hour earlier, at 4:00. The sleeping friend must have been not only saddened by the death, but also saddened that she was so tired that she fell asleep after the first message. Yet it is striking that the apparition twice had the power to interrupt such a sound sleeper. This case is interesting, too, in that the first visit must have happened an hour before the death.[3]

3. THE RED SCRATCH

In this American case, a young man had lost his eighteen year old sister, with whom he was very close. About a year after her death, this happened. Working as a salesman in St. Joseph, Missouri, he had worked the morning and returned to his hotel room to send in a large group of orders, and was pleased with his success. Thinking about his productive day, he was not thinking about his deceased sister, or about the past. It was noon and he was enjoying a cigar, and suddenly noticed someone sitting on his left side, with one arm resting on the table. The figure seems just to have appeared. Turning, he saw the face of his dead sister. Looking directly at her, he was so sure that that she was there that he leaped forward and called her by name. At this she disappeared. He reports that he was astonished, and almost doubted that the event had happened, but becoming aware of his cigar, and the paper still moist with ink, he knew he was awake. He reports that she was so close that he could have touched her, that he could see the details of her expression and her dress, and that she looked exactly as she did when alive. He even noted the kindness in the expression of her eyes, and that her skin was so lifelike that he could see the glow of moisture on its surface. Understandably, he took the next train home, and related the story to his family, with the strange detail that his sister had a bright red scratch on her face. As he said this, his mother stood, then nearly fainted, and tearfully described how, as she was with the body shortly after the death, she had accidentally scratched the girl's face, but covered it with powder. She felt badly, and had told no one of the accident, and no one had noticed the scratch under the powder. The writer relates that no one, including himself, knew of the scratch until the event of the apparition in the hotel room. The mother died some weeks later, and we might see this event as a way in which the dead sister was preparing the way for her meeting with her mother.[4]

4. A BRITISH FLIER

On November, 24, 1944, Mrs. Sokell was in bed asleep, then woke suddenly to see her son, Flight-Lieutenant Ronald Sokell standing by her bed. She reports that he looked physically solid, so she said, "Hullo, Ron." He did not answer, but appeared calm and perhaps puzzled that his father was not there. (The father, a Unitarian minister, was away on a speaking engagement.) Mrs. Sokell says that she did not feel alarm, and went back to sleep, but awoke again two hours later to see her son still there. Again she addressed him, but again he did not reply. Two days later, the Sokells received a telegram stating that their son was missing on a bombing mission from which he had not come back. Mrs. Sokell said, "I knew he would never return." [5]

5. DEATH AT SEA

Mrs. Paquet, in England, woke one morning depressed for no clear reason. Perhaps she was responding to a typical gloomy, foggy day in London. Then she had what appeared as a daytime vision of her brother standing before her, only a few feet away. He appeared with his back toward her, and was falling over a low wall. It seemed that two loops of rope were pulling him, drawing around his legs and forcing him over the wall. In response to this, Mrs. Paquet spilled her tea, clasped her face in her hands, and cried out (to herself) that her brother was drowned. Tragically, it turned out that in fact Edmund had drowned six hours before her vision, and that the accident had occurred on a ship, with tangled rope drawing around his legs, as she had seen it.[6]

6. HELP WITH FINANCES

A Mrs. P. was lying in bed waiting to feed her baby in a room lit by a lamp. Suddenly she saw a tall man, dressed in a navy officer's uniform, come to the end of the bed. Frightened, she woke her husband, who then also saw the figure. The figure spoke to her husband, in a critical manner. The defending, or perhaps defensive, husband leaped out of bed, and the figure moved away in such a manner that the light from the lamp was blocked, but then the figure disappeared into the wall. Mr. P. told his wife that the figure was that of his father, who had been dead fourteen years. Later she learned that the apparitional figure in speaking to her husband had warned him against making a poor financial decision. As it turned out, the advice was good and Mr. and Mrs. P. avoided financial catastrophe. The financial decision was a form of crisis in this case, and clear but previously unknown information was given by the apparition.[7]

7. THE TELEPHONE CALL

This remarkable report involves a crisis apparition making a telephone call. It happened to a young mother, Mrs. J.

"It was early on Thursday morning, March 6, 1969, on a cold rainy day in northwest Ohio. My husband and I were asleep when the telephone rang by my side of the bed. I answered it and heard the faint Southern voice of my mother, who lived about twelve miles away. She called me by name and said there were three things I had to do for her, or needed to know. I asked her why she sounded so weak and far away. She ignored me and proceeded to list the things that were bothering her.

One was for me to get the letters tied with a pink ribbon that were in the bottom drawer of my father's chest-of-drawers and take them outside and burn them. She then said that Peggy Jo (my younger cousin in New Jersey) was going to need my help when her husband left her and she would be crushed with his wanting a divorce. And then she said that Fanny (my deceased grandmother whom I never met) said not to worry about my gall bladder operation even though she had died from hers. She told me good-bye and that she loved me. I thought I was dreaming until my father called me about 6:00 a.m. and said, "Mama is gone!" "Gone where?" I said. He said, "I went to get her up early for a doctor's appointment and she was dead!" (My father was very stoic and relayed this to me very calmly.)

I was absolutely numb and had to call the school system where I was employed as the high school band director, to be excused for the next two days. We had a local funeral for her on Saturday, and another one in Virginia on Monday. The Tuesday after my mother was buried, my father's sister from Clarksburg, West Virginia died. She was very close to my mother and had introduced my father to my mother and had come up here for her funeral.

While my father and thirteen year old daughter were gone to West Virginia, I thought about the telephone call and went to his home to look for the letters tied with a pink ribbon. Sure enough they were there. My older sister had been married briefly before, and these were letters that her first husband (whom my mother disliked) had written her when they broke up. I burned them as instructed. Six months later my cousin's husband left her for an older wealthy woman and I tried my best to help her cope. But the biggest surprise was a successful emergency gall bladder operation I had to have the day after school was out in June.

This was really my first experience with psychic phenomena, but contact with my mother has evidenced in other ways since that telephone call from the dead. My sister, who lives in Virginia, always wondered why she wasn't contacted and I told her it was because she wouldn't have believed it."

COLLECTIVELY PERCEIVED APPARITIONS

These are apparitions that appear to more than one person at the same time and place. Skeptics of life after death have difficulty in explaining these as cases of overactive imagination, because several people are unlikely to have the same flight of imagination at the same time. These cases are quite convincing to many people.

8. WALT WHITMAN

The case occurred in Canada, and involved Horace Trauble, a friend and biographer of the American poet, Walt Whitman. Trauble was near death, and resting in the vacation lodge of Canadian friends. He was being visited by a Lt. Col. Moore Cosgrave, who gave this report. At about 3:00 a.m., Trauble became visibly weaker, almost not breathing, and seemed to be in a coma. Then he became restless, and his lips moved, and Cosgrave moved his head, thinking he needed more air. Trauble's eyes were focused on a spot about three feet above the bed, as though he were seeing something. When Cosgrave looked up, he must have been astonished. A light haze appeared, and spread until it took the form of a body. The "body" had the likeness of Walt Whitman, with tweed jacket, old felt hat, flowing hair and beard, widely spaced but rather narrow eyes, and "it" was looking down at Trauble. Whitman moved to the side of the bed, and Trauble said "There is Walt." Then, according to Cosgrave, Walt passed through the bed and seemed to touch Cosgrave's hand. The Lt. Col. reported that he felt the uncanny sensation of a low electrical charge, like one feels from a faulty electrical appliance. Then Whitman smiled at Trauble and disappeared. For a Whitman biographer, this would be an especially moving event to have happen in the last moments of life.[8]

9. AN ASTONISHED NURSE

This case occurred in New York and involved a nurse, Ms. Moser, and an elderly lady, Ms. Rosa B. Ms. Moser reports that Ms. B. was well educated, cultured, mentally competent, but very ill, and was living in a New York hotel. One afternoon Ms. B. was sleeping and Ms. Moser was sitting near her, facing the bed, and writing in her medical chart. Suddenly Ms. B. sat up, and began to wave happily. Ms. Moser turned toward the door to see who had come, and saw an elderly lady she had never seen before, who resembled the patient. Ms. Moser could see her clearly. It was full daylight and the shades were nearly completely open. The visitor walked toward the patient, bent down, and they kissed each other. Then Ms. B. took her nurse's hand, looked very pleased, and said "That is my sister." Ms. Moser reports that this happened two times later, and that Ms. B. was elated each time.[9]

10. A SPIRIT RISING

A recent report is from Tom Hurley. His mother had died, and a Catholic wake service held for her, during which the rosary was said, as she had desired. As the rosary was said, Hurley reports that he saw his mother's spirit rise from her body, the room suddenly glowing with light. This of course gave him a sense of joy, peace and wonder. After the wake, Hurley's wife Sarah asked if he had experienced anything unusual as the rosary was being read. They were surprised to find that Sarah had seen the exact same event as her husband had seen. Astonishment was added to the joy, peace and wonder.[10]

11. A LIFE-LIKE FIGURE

This case occurred in England, in a Lincolnshire farmhouse. Two young women were staying the night and sleeping in an old-fashioned four-poster bed. The bed was about four feet from the wall, and against the same wall was a cupboard. The first report is given by one of the young women, who saw, in the direction of the door of the cupboard, the face of an old lady, with a frilled white cap, and white handkerchief around her neck, a white apron, who was sitting with her hands folded in her lap. She noted that the figure appeared absolutely lifelike. Incredulous, she asked her friend, "Did you see anything?" The friend, a Miss Quilty, replied, "Did you see anything?" They then discovered they had both seen the exact same figure, and understandably had trouble sleeping the rest of the night. The next morning they discovered that they had seen a likeness of the farmer's mother, who had died in that room.[11]

12. GRANDPA BULL

In 1931, a gentleman named Samuel Bull died, and his aged wife stayed in their house with her grandson, James. A few months after the death her daughter and her daughter's husband and five children joined Mrs. Bull in the house. Five months later Mrs. Edwards (Mrs. Bull's daughter) was amazed when she saw the figure of a man climb the staircase and walk through a closed door into the room where he had died. James Bull also saw the figure, and eventually the entire family witnessed it. Mrs. Edwards' daughter, age five, was certain enough of its identity to call the figure familiarly "Grandpa Bull," and it was seen by all members of the family. When several were present, all saw the figure, so the sightings became something of a family affair. Cases like this one, involving children seeing the apparition, are quite common. Uncommon is the "intensity" of the apparition that was strong enough for all members of the family to see it. Such cases as this give evidence that these kinds of apparitions cannot easily be explained as products of hallucination or of wishful thinking.[12]

13. AN APPARITIONAL EVENT FROM THE NEW TESTAMENT

"Now that same day two of them were going to a village called Emmaus, about seven miles from Jerusalem. They were talking with each other about everything that had happened. As they talked and discussed these things with each other, Jesus himself came up and walked with them, but they were kept from recognizing him. ... As they approached the village to which they were going, Jesus acted as if he were going farther. But they urged him strongly, 'Stay with us, for it is nearly evening; the day is almost over.' So he went in to stay with them. When he was at the table with them, he broke bread, gave thanks, broke it and began to give it to them. Then their eyes were opened and they recognized him, and he disappeared from their sight." For readers who are not New Testament Scholars, or are not part of the Christian tradition, all of the post-resurrection appearances of Jesus occurred after the Crucifixion.[13]

14. A SPIRITUAL TEACHER APPEARS TO HIS PUPIL,
AND TO OTHERS IN A GROUP

Some apparitions in non-Christian cultures are also of religious figures, this one, a Hindu Holy Man who was teacher of one of the group members.

Richard Hodgson was one of the important early members of the British Society for Psychical Research. After this apparent apparitional event, Hodgson compiled written reports from several witnesses. In India, a group of people were on a balcony when an apparition appeared to several members of the group, though all did not see it. A Mr. Ramaswamier wrote that at a distance of about thirty feet, a gleaming figure assumed the shape of a man. The figure was not walking but appeared to be gliding among the upper branches of the trees, forward and backward, several times. Mr. R. did not recognize the person, whether he had a beard, whether he was tall or not. There was moonlight, and the time was between 8:00 and 9:00 p.m. Surprised by this, he must have been dumbfounded when he discovered that a number of people in his group had seen the same figure.

Similar written accounts were given by Mr. Ramaswamier, District Registrar of Madura, Mr. Nobin Krishna Bannerji, Manager General of Ward's Estates in Moorshedabad, Mr. Chandra Sekhara, Teacher in High School in Bareilly, Mr. J.N. Ghosal, and Mr. Norendra Nath Sen, Editor of *The Indian Mirror*. The reports are almost identical, but with minor differences in detail. This case is similar to the New Testament report of the disciples' experience on the road to Emmaus, quoted above. The figure was seen, but not recognized by some, and then it "vanished." [14]

APPARITIONS OF THE DEAD

Apparitions of the dead are designated by some researchers as apparitions that occur more than twelve hours after the death, as opposed to crisis apparitions that occur less than twelve hours after the death. Some of these are also collectively perceived cases.

15. A BALANCE OF SKEPTICISM AND OPENNESS

A dentist reports: "On the ninth day after my mother's funeral, I was at home alone. I was not busy at that moment and it was a beautiful winter day. I had opened the front door to let the sun in, and Daisy, our golden retriever, was sitting in the sunlight inside the door. I was just sitting there and I sensed some movement. At first I thought it was Daisy, but when I looked she was sitting quietly warming herself in the sunlight. The sense of movement was followed by a sense of the stillness of the air, then a sense of my skin crawling, like goose-bumps around my upper left arm and neck. My reaction was to deny it, but then I began to ask myself, 'Is it possible this could be Mom?' It was all momentary, then I thought, 'I don't need to be afraid of this, or be in denial or fearful. I just need to dwell with this notion.' Then I had a sense that if it is Mom, she's letting me know that she is O.K, perhaps letting me know that she is my advocate, that I don't need to be fearful. After about a minute the sensation in my arm stopped. Then I looked again at Daisy and she had not moved. Nothing like this has ever happened before, except that with other deaths in the family I have had a sense of the spirit hovering around shortly after the death. I don't know whether the feeling is a sense of unity of spirit, or that in dealing with loss, the deceased person is actually there on our behalf. A friend who has done some research said that Robert Crookall found that elderly people who die of natural causes are often too depleted to communicate until some weeks or months after the death. But then I thought – 'Well, Mom has a mind of her own, so maybe she is here.'"

16. ALTERING A WILL

This case is well known by researchers, and was, like many of the others in this collection, investigated by the American Society for Psychical Research. A Mr. J.P. Chaffin had lost his father to death four years previously, but had dreamed on a number of occasions that his father appeared at his bedside. At the time of death, apparently the elder Chaffin had left a will dividing his estate among his other children, but had excluded his son, J.P. Chaffin. Mr. Chaffin may have felt resentful, or perhaps sad, that his father had not included him in the will, but the final dream was instructive. In the last dream, the father was wearing an old overcoat, and told his son that he would find a will in the overcoat pocket. Mr. Chaffin searched the pocket of the coat (since the father's death it had hung in a closet) and found a roll of paper which revealed the location of the second will. Whatever emotions the younger Mr. Chaffin had experienced must have turned to elation when the second will was probated and the court redistributed the inheritance accordingly.[15]

17. HE APPEARED SOLID

A business executive reported that, following the death of her father, she was feeling quite despondent. On the night before the funeral, she was in a hotel with her five year old son and a friend. She reports that as she was praying, the lights became dim, and suddenly she saw her father. He appeared solid, and about twenty years younger than he had been in physical life. There were colors radiating around him, and he asked his daughter to care for her mother, and told her he loved her. The five year old, whom the mother thought was asleep, got up and said "My granddaddy! My granddaddy!" Deeply moved, the mother told him that granddaddy was gone, but the boy insisted that granddaddy was in the room with them. This apparition was perceived by two people.[16]

18. PALLADIA

One of Gurney's cases came from Russia. A gentleman, Eugene Mamtchich, wrote that he had known a girl named Palladia, who, sadly, had died at age fifteen. He communicated "by alphabet" with the girl, who told him to replace an angel, which was falling. Most likely with some doubt, he went to the cemetery, dug in the snow and found her grave, with its marble angel and cross that were falling, and set them upright. Perhaps appreciative, Palladia appeared to him and to his wife several times, and to their small son. On one occasion when she appeared, a dog ran in fright. On another occasion Palladia said that she felt peace in the place where she was, and reassured Eugene's wife that she, the apparition, was "good, and affectionate." [17]

19. ANN VISITS HARRIET

Myers cites a case in which two female cousins had been summoned to the sick bed of an aunt. The aunt, named Harriet, had been extremely close to her sister, Ann, who had died six years previously. The cousins were awake at about 1:00 a.m., and saw someone pass the door. The figure was short, wrapped in a shawl, had a wig with three curls on each side, and a black cap. Amazed but apparently not speechless, one cousin called to the other that it was Aunt Ann, and the response came that, yes it was Aunt Ann, and that Harriet would die that day. Another family member also saw the apparition, and indeed, Aunt Harriet died at 6:00 p.m. that day. (We may expect that the two cousins for the rest of their lives took the sighting of apparitions very seriously.)[18]

20. SMOKEY THE CAT

This is one of many investigated cases of an animal apparition, especially interesting in that there were a number of human observers, at the same time and place. Two sisters both saw through a window their cat Smokey walk across the lawn. One of the sisters even noticed that it had a characteristic limp. A few minutes later Smokey was seen by one of the sisters and a friend, from the same window. With no reason to suspect anything unusual, they hunted for the cat, but as happens so often with cats, it could not be found. Later in the day, a servant saw the cat, and offered it a drink of milk, which the cat ignored. It turned out that Smokey was actually already dead at the times he was seen, and it was proved when the gardener exhumed the body from under a tree where Smokey had recently been buried.[19]

21. CARE FOR THE GRANDCHILDREN

A Ms. Dodson reports that on a Sunday evening, between eleven and twelve at night, she heard her name being called, three times. At first she thought it was her uncle, but on the third call, recognized the voice of her mother, who had been dead for sixteen years. Ms. Dodson must have been startled, for she said "Momma!" and a figure came around a screen near her bed with two children. The figure placed the children in Ms. Dodson's arms and instructed her that she must care for them as their mother had recently died. The figure twice extracted a promise, then disappeared. Ms. Dodson felt the children in her arms, then fell asleep. In the morning there was no evidence of the night's events, but on Tuesday morning Ms. Dodson received word that her sister-in-law had died. Ms. Dodson must have been thunderstruck, for she had not known of the birth of the youngest child, three weeks before. [20] (Apparitions sometimes do appear in dreams, as in the Yellow Door event in Chapter Two and in the Chaffin case above.)

22. A BLUE VELVET DRESS

A modern and moving event happened to Tricia, a clothing designer in Florida. Soon after her mother's death, the writer was in her bedroom, and suddenly felt a presence. Turning on a small night light, she saw her mother, standing, in a blue velvet dress Tricia had never seen. The mother had died of cancer, weighing only fifty seven pounds, but the apparition looked healthy and happy. Tricia was overjoyed, and ran into the other room to tell her family, but they thought she was just being excitable, and finally calmed her down. Some time later, as Tricia and her aunt were going through her mother's things, they came across a blue velvet dress, and Tricia began to cry. The aunt asked what was wrong, but the tears were tears of joy. Tricia told her this was the dress her mother had on when Tricia had seen her. As if further confirmation were needed, the aunt then reported that the blue velvet dress was her mother's wedding dress, that her mother had made it herself, being unable to afford a commercially made one.[21]

HAUNTING APPARITIONS

The strongest haunting cases occur repeatedly, to several people in the same location, and the figures often show similar behavior. There are many popular collections of "ghost stories," but relatively few of the reports involve several people independently seeing the same events, and few have been investigated or carefully described as in scholarly journals. Some of these reports involved several people, and were investigated and/or written up in the journals of the British or American Societies for Psychical Research. The interpretation of the events has of course given rise to different theories.

This report was obtained by the author, after a newspaper solicitation. He visited the house and room in question, but experienced no unusual feelings or events.

23. THE HAIR ON MY FRIEND'S ARM STOOD UP

Andrea, a twenty-nine year old married mother of two, moved with her family into a house in 1997. Previously it had been lived in for sixty years by an elderly woman who had died there in her sleep, accompanied by a nurse at her bedside. Andrea reports several different kinds of peculiar events, beginning when she moved into the house, and continuing to the present.

When the family first moved into the house, everyone noticed that a bedroom in the back of the house seemed always cold, and friends and family members thought perhaps it had not been properly insulated by previous owners. The windows were hard to open, and Andrea felt uncomfortable in the room, so would wait in another part of the house for her husband to come home after working second shift. Once a friend said the hair on her arm stood up when she went into that room. Andrea found herself talking to the previous owner as if she were in the house, and asked her to leave. "The room stopped being cold after that." It is not unusual for observers to report a feeling of coldness in haunting cases.

On one occasion, in 2003, Andrea was cleaning house during the day, and when she reached for the phone, her wind chimes began to play. The chimes were about four feet away from her. She says that the chimes are electrical and have a cord, but it was unplugged. It happened again, she says, on a day that her furnace was being repaired, and "...the furnace blew up." The repairman said there was "no way" that the furnace would blow up that way, but the company replaced the furnace anyway, at their expense. This occurred some years after the back bedroom began not to be cold, according to Andrea. Strange electrical events are not unusual in the literature on apparitions, and the last case report in this chapter, "A Lively Gift Shop" also reports them.

In one of the strangest events, Andrea reports that she woke one night and, walking to her kitchen, saw a little girl dressed in a long pink gown. She thought it was her two year-old daughter and called out to her, but the figure did not answer, and "...moved further away until she was gone." Andrea says, "I then went to my daughter's room and found her sleeping." This is interesting especially in that there seemed to be no reason why Andrea would be even thinking about her daughter, much less worried about her. In fact she logically assumed that it was her daughter but then found her daughter asleep and well.

Andrea also reports that at night she has wakened to see "blob-like figures" and that they were "not solid." They would frighten her, and then they would just disappear. Sometimes it seemed something was crouching over her bed, about three feet away. After a while, she says, she became tired of the figures, and said to them that she did not want them to appear anymore, and they stopped. (Opaque, blob-like figures are not unusual in reports on apparitions.)

24. A FEARLESS LIBRARIAN

A librarian had very recently taken his new job, and had not seen a photograph of this face he soon observed. As he was leaving his office in the library, he was astonished to see a man's face at the far end of a narrow passage. Warily thinking that perhaps a thief had entered late in the day, he put down the books and picked up a revolver. But moving toward the place where he thought the thief could be hiding, he found nothing. By this time he was in the main room of the library, a large space that contained a number of bookcases. Then he saw a face looking "round" one of the bookcases, appearing as if the body were inside the bookcase, but no figure could be seen. The face was without hair, pale, and the eyes were deeply set. As he walked toward the face, the body seemed to "rotate" out of the bookcase and an old man with high shoulders walked in a shuffling gait to a small bathroom. The librarian maintained his courage. The bathroom had no other access, but when the librarian followed the figure into the bathroom, again no one was there. The next morning, when he let the story of this strange happening slip to a local clergyman, and described the figure, the pastor said, "Why, that's Old Q." Later, the librarian was shown a picture that matched the figure he had seen, and he must have been amazed to learn that this man had lost his hair from a gunpowder accident, and had died previously, at about the same time of year.[22]

25. A JUDGMENTAL FAMILY

A Mrs. M. reports that, previous to this event, she and her husband had no idea that the house they were living in had anything unusual about it, or that the family who had lived there previously had suffered such great turmoil. At about 11:00 p.m., Mrs. M. reports that she heard a moaning sound, as

A judgmental family

though someone were in great distress. She was naturally concerned, and looking out the window, she saw on the grass a beautiful young girl kneeling before an officer, crying, and clasping her hands together as if asking for forgiveness. Callously, the officer waved her away, and Mrs. M. went outside to ask the girl to come in. The figures dissolved, and Mrs. M. immediately wrote in a diary what she had seen, and the date. As it turned out, the youngest daughter of previous owners, perhaps a self-righteous family, had become pregnant and delivered a child. Her parents and relatives were unsympathetic and would not recognize her, or the child, and she had died alone in sorrow. The soldier, a distinguished officer, was apparently a close relative, and she also had not been able to gain his forgiveness. Later, Mrs. M. was amazed when she recognized the soldier, a General, from a portrait hung in the home of an acquaintance, and the host of the house where the portrait hung confirmed that indeed it was the same person.[23]

26. THE CHELTENHAM HAUNTING

This is probably the most widely known and widely discussed case of haunting, at least in the western hemisphere. It is convincing to many scholars of psychic research, and was written up in the *Proceedings* of the British Society for Psychical Research.

Rose Despard, an English medical student, and her sisters, (and sometimes other people) saw a figure that appeared as a tall woman dressed in black. The figure disturbed dogs, and showed awareness of humans by avoiding being touched. Some people saw the apparition during the day and it was apparently so solid that they mistook it for a flesh and blood person. One guest asked who the woman in the other room was, and the woman turned out to be the apparition. The SPR discovered that neighbors and even casual visitors saw the figure, and that people actually became accustomed to seeing it. Once, in play, a group of children formed a ring around the apparition, at which time it disappeared. The reports sound as though it had simply become a matter of fact that people would see the figure when they came near the Despard house. The Despard family, who reported the events, were apparently reliable and of good reputation, and believed the figure to be the second wife of a previous owner of the house. In a rather tragic story, the previous residents had been heavy drinkers, and there was a divorce, with the death of both husband and wife within a short time. Rose Despard saw a picture of the woman and, after all that had happened, was probably not surprised when she was able to identify her as the figure in black.[24]

27. THE GRAY LADY AND THE DYING

In 1956 a nurse, E.L., was making rounds in a London hospital, filling the water dispensers at each patient's bedside. As she began filling the dispenser for one patient, the elderly man told her that she need not fill it as he had already been given a glass of water. Thinking that there were no other nurses pouring water, E.L. asked him who had given him the water. He replied that a nice lady, dressed in gray, standing at the foot of the bed, had given him the water. E.L. could see no one else in the room, and the man died a week later. E.L. also must have been very curious about what all of this meant.

E.L. signed the account of this event, and a physician, Dr. Paul Turner, recognized the importance of the account. He began an investigation of a legend to the effect that in this particular ward of the hospital, a lady in gray often appeared to dying patients. The nurses in this hospital had at one time worn gray, but had discontinued that uniform in the 1920s and the new uniform was a blue dress with white apron and collar.

Turner published the results of his investigation in the *Journal of the Society for Psychical Research*, with six separate accounts from nurses of encounters with the gray lady. Other accounts were not written down, and so not included in the report.

Nurse J.F.K. signed a statement that she was bathing a patient in 1956, when the patient asked her if she always worked with the other nurse. No other nurse was with her, and when she asked the patient what he meant, the patient pointed at what he was seeing. Nurse J.F.K. could see no one, and must have been quite puzzled. But the patient said that this nurse dressed differently from the other nurses, and that she came frequently to visit him. He died shortly afterward.

Nurse J.M.P. signed a statement that in 1957 a patient asked her, "Who is that lady warming her hands by the fire?" Asked what he saw, he said, "That person in the gray uniform." He closed his eyes and soon expired.

In 1958, Nurse S.T. reported that a patient had told her during the night that a kind lady dressed in gray had given her a cup of tea.

In 1959, Nurse R.A.C. reported that a patient told her that a kind lady was standing at the foot of her bed during the night.

Sister E.F. signed a statement that when she asked a dying patient if she could make her more comfortable, the patient said that the other sister had already done so. No other sister was on duty at the time, and the night nurse had not attended to the patient recently.

We are not told how the nurses reacted emotionally to these strange encounters. But it is not hard to imagine goose bumps, hair raising on the back of the neck, prickly skin, trembling, doubt of their own sanity, panic, or maybe the calmness of having received confirmation of what they already believed.

We are also not told whether nurses, knowing these stories, preferred to work, or not to work, on this particular ward. Concerning medication as a possible trigger for the events, the investigators said that only some of the patients were receiving medication, but there is no known medication that would make a number of patients hallucinate the same figure. Also, such events occurred only on this particular ward of this hospital, and not in other wards, or in other hospitals treating patients with the same kinds of disorders. If somehow the nurses had conspired to fabricate these stories, we might expect their statements to be substantially alike, but they are not. The investigators also say that although there was something of a legend about the "gray lady" in the hospital, this was a secret carefully kept from the patients. It seems unlikely that such a legend could be kept secret, but even if it was known to some patients, that knowledge does not explain the consistency of events happening to dying elderly people.[25]

28. THE GRASS LAKE ENCOUNTER

This recent case is one of many that can be found reported by local societies who investigate and then describe cases to their members. This case is described on the internet.

Dennis Hauck writes that in 1973, three families living around a small lake in Illinois were calling the local fire departments and police reporting strange orange lights in the sky. Soon, poltergeist-like events began happening, with lights blinking on and off, loud sounds, foul odors, radios turning on and off by themselves, personal objects disappearing then reappearing. The phenomena then gradually became more like apparitions: one woman said she mistook a shadowy figure for her husband; the figure walked around the bed, and when she reached for the light, it disappeared. A young girl reported that something pulled the covers down to her knees and pinched her toes. She must have been frightened, as she said she felt a coldness just before and during the event. Some years later, when Hauck visited the house where this happened, when he left, his car lights began blinking on and off, and the next day a mechanic could find no reason for this to happen. They did discover that the left side of the car was "magnetized" and a geiger counter in the trunk was ruined, though it had not been turned on. Eventually, one woman had a nervous breakdown, there was a divorce and considerable family conflict, and a church group was warning that the residents had brought "demons" into their house and began performing exorcisms. (More follow-up would have been fascinating, but Dennis Hauck does not in this article report any final outcome.) [26]

29. A HAUNTED PARSONAGE

An Anglican priest and his wife had moved into the first parish to which they had been appointed. On the second night, after sleeping for several hours, they heard a crash that sounded like iron bars falling to the ground. The local woman whom they had hired also heard it. But this was only the beginning: the sound occurred repeatedly during their first year, always at 2:00 a.m. on Sunday morning. This is not the time of the week that a priest needs to hear an apparition! The local woman said she had heard that such things happened in that house, and, probably wisely, chose to sleep in her own house from that time on. Apparently undaunted, the priest and his wife began to hear heavy footsteps, but they still could find nothing. After that, they began to hear sounds as of heavy boxes being tossed around in their attic, but investigation showed nothing out of place. Though some people would have been terrorized, the pastor and his wife began to address the agent, telling it to be quiet, or to come out and be more straightforward, but this always led to louder and more persistent noises. The priest wrote lovingly about his two Skye terriers, who were excellent watchdogs, but always cowered when these events happened. The priest discussed the events with a neighbor woman, who informed him that the house was locally regarded as haunted.[27]

30. APPARITIONS OF THE VIRGIN MARY

According to the Marian Apparition Directory, there have been 386 reported cases of Marian apparitions in the Twentieth Century. In 299 of the cases, the Roman Catholic Church has made no decision regarding the supernatural character of the apparitions. In 79 cases, a negative decision was made, and in 8 cases the church has analyzed and decided that supernatural events were occurring. These are important, as millions of faithful people are visiting shrines and other sites of the appearances, and Catholic ideas about communicating with the saints are not far removed from these apparitional events.[28]

One example is Medjugorje (now Bosnia). Six young adults had a vision of Our Lady in 1981. Two of them were taking a walk and saw a figure bathed in light, floating above the ground, who later identified herself as the Queen of Peace. The vision lasted about thirty minutes, and four other young people then joined. From that time, the visions have continued, with other people seeing the figure, and with the figure giving messages that have been widely shared, especially in Catholic circles. The original visionaries report that the apparition is a three-dimensional figure, real and solid, has dark hair, blue eyes, wears a gray dress and crown, and appears about nineteen years old. There have been numerous messages through the years.[29]

The last message, posted March 25, 2004, is as follows: "Dear children! Also today, I call you to open yourselves to prayer. Especially now, in this time of grace, open your hearts, little children, and express your love to the Crucified. Only in this way, will you discover peace, and prayer will begin to flow from your heart into the world. Be an example, little children, and an incentive for the good. I am close to you and I love you all. Thank you for having responded to my call." [30]

In the Medjugorje case, there have been interesting medical and psychological findings. For example, one researcher discovered that when the visionaries were seeing the apparition, the corneal eye reflex was absent, so that a blinding light did not cause them to blink, as it did before and after the events. Eyelid movements were slower during the events, and electro-oculogram readings showed that the visionaries reacted to the appearance of the apparition simultaneously with one another to within one-tenth to four-tenths of a second. Eye and muscular movements resumed at precisely the same time when the appearance ended.

During the visions, the eyes of the visionaries converged on the same point in space, the point at which they said they were seeing the apparition.[31]

31. A LIVELY GIFT SHOP

This case is an example of a modern, carefully investigated poltergeist event. Poltergeist events, in which objects are moved, or electronic gadgets manipulated, or sounds produced or apparitions seen, can usually be traced to living agents, often emotionally upset people associated with the place. But in about 25% of cases there is no living agent that can be identified, and researchers in cases like this believe that the agent is deceased.

Karlis Osis, then Research Director of the American Society for Psychical Research, and an associate, Donna McCormick, were called by the owner of a gift shop in an old house in southern New Jersey in 1979. Over a period of about ten years, and through three sets of owners, electronic devices had been turned on and off, objects were moved, sounds were heard, and an occasional apparition was seen.

At least twenty four people had independently reported these events, with varying knowledge of their having occurred earlier. Some events were experienced by several people at the same time.

Cautious that the owner of the store might be seeking publicity to boost business, the researchers waited several months before beginning an investigation and learned that the events had not been reported to newspapers or other media, and had, in fact, begun before the old house was used as a business. The researchers found that the reports were too consistent and from too many diverse people (some former employees) to have been a hoax, and that the owners themselves had nothing to gain but rather something to lose, from creating such a story for publicity purposes.

The events, which happened about once a month, included movement of a table to a place it had occupied when two sisters lived there. One sister had died in 1949, the other in 1954. Movement of objects in the gift shop began about 1978. This included a scattering of tools from a tabletop while an electrician was working, repeated opening of a filing cabinet drawer that normally stayed shut by itself, a falling florescent light, slamming of a door, chiming of an unwound grandfather clock, playing of unwound music boxes, electronic equipment starting and stopping by itself, an adding machine beginning by itself to print out zeros, an alarm system going off when no one was present, even though it was replaced three times.

There were flapping noises, a crash, a knock, and on one occasion when they challenged the "ghost" there was immediately a pounding that lasted 30-45 seconds. There were footsteps reported by twelve of the individuals interviewed, and some reported voices that sounded like a party was going on when there was no one in the shop. A surveillance camera showed nothing but an empty room.

Apparitions were usually in the form of moving shadows, but one report was of a clear impression of an elderly woman in a plain housedress with gray hair piled on top of her head. One witness reported that in 1976 a hand had pushed her down one step. After hitting her back on the corner of the stairs, she went to the hospital and found that several vertebrae were knocked out of place. Through the years, this is the only report of an event in which the supposed poltergeist acted with malice.

Careful checks of the electrical system showed nothing to explain the events, and there were none of the twenty four witnesses who could be identified as always present when things began to happen.

Eighteen of the witnesses said they had had no paranormal experiences outside of the gift shop, so the only common denominator for these events seemed to be the house itself. Of the original family members who had lived in the house, the events seemed to fit the dynamic and self-assertive personality of

Hester (d. 1949) rather than the meek-mannered Lucille (d. 1954). Carlton, a cousin of the sisters, (d. 1934) who had lived next door, and Arthur Maxwell (d. 1970), a nephew of the sisters, had reportedly not shown much interest in the house. The sisters, however, reportedly were deeply attached to it.

Osis and McCormick made three trips to the gift shop, and took with them a different psychic each time. Before the psychics had any contact with gift shop personnel, they tape recorded their impressions. Only one of the psychics had impressions that seemed, according to neighbors who had known them, to fit the personality of any of the previous occupants. I.B. considered a woman to be the prominent figure, and according to those who knew her, gave an accurate impression of her physical appearance. I.B. had the impression that this woman was proud of their lifestyle, was a "leading citizen," but was concerned that her family had "sunk very low" and was degraded because they had to "go for subsidies." Neighbors confirmed that the sisters were very proud and were quite embarrassed to have to receive public relief toward the end of their lives. I.B. had the impression that one of the sisters was concerned to defend the family name and the integrity of the house, and was "lingering" there to act as a poltergeist agent. According to I.B., the house became run down, slanderous stories circulated, and one of the sisters had been concerned to have them corrected. According to one neighbor, cruel rumors were in fact spread during his childhood about the "spinster sisters," and people would cross to the other side of the street when passing the house.

There is a great deal of research literature about poltergeist events, and this case, while not convincing to everyone, is quite suggestive, and demonstrates modern techniques of research.[32]

DISCUSSION
SOME STATISTICS

In 1973 Andrew Greely conducted a remarkable survey. He asked subjects if they ever felt that they were really in touch with someone who had died. He found that 27% of his subjects overall answered yes, and that 51% of widows and widowers answered affirmatively. (32) At about the same time, in England, W.D. Rhys found similar results: 47% reported contact with the dead, 39% felt a presence, 14% saw a presence, 13% heard a presence, 12% talked to the presence, and 3% touched the presence.[33]

In a somewhat different kind of survey, Ian Stevenson found that when two or more people are present, 2/3 of the time two or more people will experience the apparition. Another study showed that 56% of apparitional events, overall, are collectively perceived. 78% of apparitional events involve people who had close emotional ties, and of 314 cases, Ian Stevenson found that 52% of the apparitional events followed a violent death.[34]

CHARACTERISTICS OF APPARITIONS: PHYSICAL AND NONPHYSICAL

Apparitions have both physical and non-physical characteristics, sometimes occurring in the same event. Thousands of apparitions cases have been studied, and physical features include the following. On some occasions, the apparition appears opaque, and is reflected in mirrors. Apparitions adapt to situations, for example, walking around tables, or people, or appearing in the same place repeatedly. At times people will also walk around apparitions, they are so realistic in appearance. They may be seen from different perspectives by different people. Sporadically, apparitions move objects or switch electrical gadgets off and on. Animals will sometimes react to apparitions, and usually apparitions wear clothes! Apparitions can at times be felt, smelled, and heard, as well as seen.[35]

Non-physical characteristics include the following. Apparitions sometimes appear as a ball of light, and glide rather than to walk, or they go through walls or doors without opening them, and from time to time make a sudden appearance, rather than a normal approach. They are seen by some people, but not by others, and are not always recognized. Often they "vanish" as quickly as they appear.

THEORIES TO EXPLAIN APPARITIONS

These characteristics have given rise to several theories about what is actually happening in an apparitional event.

The most common theory among skeptics can be called the "Vivid Imagination Theory." According to this theory, people wish to have reassurance that their loved ones are not really gone. As real as they may seem, these apparitions are created in the minds of percipients, and have no other reality. They may offer excitement, comfort, or even information that was lying dormant in the unconscious mind of the percipient. This no doubt describes some apparitional events, but is not likely to explain all. One kind of event not explained this way is the collective apparition, where several people see the same event, apparently independently. We have seen that there are many such cases.

Another theory has been called the "Hallucination Theory." This does not imply mental illness, but suggests that the deceased person triggers a "hallucination" or vision in a normal person or group. This theory would require that observers receive a telepathic message from the deceased. This theory may work for some kinds of events, such as that in which the deceased is wearing clothes. According to this theory the percipient receives the message from the deceased, then "rounds out" the experience by mentally creating clothes for the apparition to wear! The theory assumes that the deceased can give a verifiable message (one that turns out to be "true") through telepathy, and that the recipient can receive it telepathically. A serious problem with this theory is that few people display any great telepathic ability. Such events as the Chaffin Will case, (number 23) and the British Pilot case (number 4) would require a talent that could only be described as super ESP.

The "Spirit Theory" seems better to some researchers. According to this theory, "something" actually leaves the body of the deceased but continues to live, and it has a physical or semi-physical quality. With *purposeful* apparitions, it seems more reasonable to think that "something" is acting with a purpose. With *collectively perceived* apparitions, it seems simpler to think that "something" is actually present in a group, whose members see it as opaque, or from different perspectives, or not at all.

APPARITIONS AND RELIGIOUS FAITH

This "something" has been called "soul" or "spirit" in many different religions and cultures. Since the writer's tradition is Christian, we will explore briefly the implications for Christian faith. But a writer from another tradition could as easily relate these findings about apparitions to her own tradition.

St. Paul referred to a "spiritual body" in I Corinthians 15. He distinguished it from a physical body. Some of the reports of those who said they saw the risen Christ sound like they saw a more physical form, such as the Jesus who ate fish with the disciples at the Sea of Tiberias, or in the upper room where, according to John, Jesus said "Touch me not..." Other reports sound more like non-physical appearances, such as Paul's report that Jesus "appeared" to him on the Road to Damascus, or the report that the Disciples saw him in the upper room, or on the Road to Emmaus, where they did not even recognize him.

The differences in these reports in the New Testament have contributed to the differences among theologians and lay people over the nature of Jesus' and our own resurrections. Most conservative people hold fast to an expectation of a physical resurrection only at the end of time. More liberal people tend to think of a more spiritual kind of resurrection as an ongoing event, in which the risen Christ is available to us as to the Disciples after the resurrection, and that our own life after death happens for believers at the time of or shortly after the death of the physical body.

It seems clear that the study of life after death research, and especially of apparitions, can contribute to a deepening of religious faith for many people of many different traditions. This perspective reminds us that materialism as a philosophy is not the last word, has become more shaky in recent years, and does not explain many important events that occur in the world. It also reminds us that the Resurrection of Jesus was most likely an event that had an objective reality, as well as a subjective reality in the minds of the early Christians. In view of the research, it is very unlikely that the early Christians were simply imagining the presence of Jesus, and it is unlikely that Jesus' appearances prove either that his resurrection was only physical or only spiritual. The research and the New Testament support each other in showing that something profoundly real is involved in our experience of meeting the risen Christ, and in our expectation of a resurrection following our own physical death.

For a fuller treatment of Biblical, theological, and parapsychological considerations of life after death, see the author's earlier book, *What Happens When I Die? A Study of Life After Death.*

VALIDATION OF APPARITIONS CASES

This dizzying array of findings is only the tip of the iceberg of serious studies on apparitions. This research has been pursued for over one hundred years in a systematic way. Early researchers included Edmund Gurney, F.W.H. Myers, Camille Flammarion, Mrs. Sedgwick, Frank Podmore, Reverend Thomas Drayton, Dr. Oliver Lodge, William James and Richard Hodgson of the British and American Societies for Psychical Research. This was in many ways the heyday of apparitions research, and many of the cases included in this collection are from the work of these researchers. They are strong cases, and are referred to frequently by the serious modern researchers such as Raymond Bayless, Alan Gauld, Ian Currie and others.

However, illustrious names do not prove the authenticity of a single case. They only suggest that careful and intelligent people have found the cases to be worthy of study. The more open minded people study the evidence, the more they become confident that the arguments skeptics offer are not well founded.

AN ANSWER TO SKEPTICS OF LIFE AFTER DEATH

Robert Almeder[36] has written perhaps the clearest recent defense against skeptical criticism of the evidence for life after death. While a reasonable dose of skepticism is appropriate for assessing these case studies, hyper-skepticism does not contribute to truth or to understanding. Almeder is a professional philosopher of science. Because of the importance and strength of his argument with skeptics who claim science as a reason for not accepting the considerable evidence supporting life after death, we will present a summary here of his thoughts.

1. Most skeptics argue on the ground that the idea of a personality existing independently of a physical body is inconceivable. Since we cannot imagine what disembodied life would be like, skeptics say, there is no sense even in talking about it.

   The skeptic's mistake is in assuming that our inability to imagine something means that it cannot exist. The basis for our belief or disbelief that disembodied persons cannot exist should be based on whether we have sufficient evidence, not on whether we can imagine them as we would imagine a physical object.

2. The second common skeptical objection to belief in life after death is the argument that there is no evidence for life after death that will hold up under serious modern scientific scrutiny. This view is based on the belief that apparitions of the dead are not publicly repeatable in experimental situations under controlled conditions. It also considers that apparitions and other paranormal reports are "anecdotal" and therefore a belief that they are real cannot be a firm item of human knowledge.

   As a philosopher of science, Almeder points out that it is a mistake to think that all knowledge requires publicly repeatable evidence. Such repeatability is necessary only when we need to know WHY a thing happens. It is not necessary to know WHY an event happens in order to know THAT indeed it did happen. For instance, we do not need repeatable experiments concerning the past existence of dinosaurs, or the past activity of the planets for us to know that indeed dinosaurs lived, or that planets have a long and complex history. In fact, concerning life after death, we do have repeatable and public evidence. That is the value of the case studies in this book. The fact that such events are not repeatable at will is not evidence that they do not happen.

3. The third common skeptical objection to belief in life after death is the belief that only if hoax or fraud are clearly ruled out can we be persuaded of life after death. In any case study, how do we know for certain that the writer, or the subject, is telling the truth about what actually happened, or

that her perception of what happened was not seriously distorted?

First, we need to admit clearly and openly that psychical research has **indeed** been victimized by unscrupulous and fraudulent people. A rehearsal of the exposures of fraudulent mediums and others since the beginning of organized research would take a volume in itself. Colin Wilson, in *Afterlife,* has given a summary of these disastrous escapades that have made many skeptical of the whole field of psychical research. It needs to be said, though, that psychical researchers themselves have been mortified and have participated fully in exposing fraud in their own field. Also, in fairness, it is also true that other fields of research, perhaps every other field, has had its own charlatans that have been exposed. Genuinely thoughtful people will not disregard **all** research in an entire field of study because some participants have been found to be fraudulent.

We need only point to the best and strongest cases, such as those in this collection, and note that these kinds of cases have occurred in all times and places, and that many logically identical cases continue to occur regularly. They are also reported independently, so for all of these reasons they provide a form of the repeatability rightly prized in scientific research. And when so many thousands of cases occur, with such consistent patterns, and so many researchers cannot discover hoax or fraud, the chances of hoax or fraud become more and more remote.

In summary, it has not been shown that any of these cases are fraudulent. For all the reasons listed above, we also believe that most are not attributable to coincidence, misreporting, hallucination, drugs, or mental or physical problems. So we believe that skeptics have a very hard argument to make. People who take the time to study the evidence with an open mind leave much of their skepticism behind.

FOOTNOTES

1. Colin Wilson, *Afterlife*, Harrap Press, London, 1987, page 129.
2. Cited by Ian Currie, *You Cannot Die,* Somerville House, Toronto, 1998. pages 3-4.
3. Camille Flammarion, cited by Raymond Bayless, *Apparitions and Survival of Death,* Citadel Press, New York, 1973, page 151.
4. F.W.H. Myers, *Human Personality and Its Survival of Bodily Death,* Hampton Roads Publishing, Charlottesville, VA, 2001, pages 181-184.
5. Currie, *Op. Cit.,* pages 20-21.
6. Cited by Currie, *Op.Cit.,* page 21.
7. Cited by Alan Gauld, *Mediumship and Survival,* Heinemann, London, 1982, pages 234-235.
8. Cited by Currie, *Op. Cit.,* pages 178-179.
9. *Ibid.,* pages 178-180.

10 Cited by Louis LaGrand, *After Death Communications*, Llewellyn Publications, St. Paul, MN, 1998, pages 55-56.

11. Gauld, *Op. Cit.,* page 237.

12. Cited by *Bayless Op.Cit.,* pages 30-31.

13. *Luke* 24:13-16,28-31, *New International Version.*

14. From "Astral Apparitions of the Mahatmas at Bombay," compiled by Richard Hodgson, at www.blavatskyarchives.com.

15. Cited by Gauld, *Op. Cit.,* page 233.

16. Bill Guggenheim and Judy Guggenheim, *Hello From Heaven,* Bantam Books, New York, 1995, pages 328-329.

17. Cited by Myers, *Op. Cit.,* page 176.

18. *Ibid.,* pages 182-183.

19. Bayless, *Op. Cit.,* pages 62-63.

20. Cited by Myers, *Op. Cit.,* page 185.

21. Bill Guggenheim and Judy Guggenheim, *Op. Cit.,* pages 280-*281.*

22. Myers, *Op. Cit.,* page 204.

23. *Ibid.,* page 207.

24. Melvin Morse, *Where God Lives,* Cliff Street Books, New York, 2000, pages 82-83.

25. Robert Almeder, *Death And Personal Survival,* Roman Littlefield, Lanham, MD, 1992, pages 106-107.

26. Dennis Hauck, www.hauntedplaces.com.

27. Ian Currie, *Op. Cit.,* pages 44-49.

28. From "Marian Apparitions of the Twentieth Century," at www.udayton.edu/mary/resources/aprtable.html.

29. Michael Durham, *Miracles of Mary,* Blackberry Press, New York, 1995, pages 25-28.

30. http://www.marysource.com/Medjugorje/medugorje_msg.htm.

31. Michael Carroll, *Medjugorje: Facts, Documents, Theology,* Veritas Publications, Dublin, 1989, pages 64-70.

32. "A Poltergeist Case Without an Identifiable Living Agent," by Karlis Osis and Donna McCormack, *Journal of the American Society for Psychical Research,* June, 1982, Volume 76, Number 1, pages 23-24.

33. Andrew Greely, *The Sociology of the Paranormal,* Russell Sage Foundation, New York, 1975.

34. From Howard A. Mickel, "How the Academic World Perceives Psychic Research," in "Proceedings of the 1981 Annual Conference of the Academy of Religion and Psychical Research," page 11.

35. "The Contribution of Apparitions to the Evidence for Survival," by Ian Stevenson, in *Journal of the American Society for Psychical Research,* October, 1982, Volume 76, Number 4, page 349.

36. Almeder, *Op. Cit.*

CHAPTER SEVEN

REINCARNATION

"What do I say when my grandson talks
about having lived before? We don't believe
in reincarnation."

A Grandmother from Maine

In 1633, one of the greatest scandals in Christendom occurred when the Church tried and condemned Galileo without really studying his telescope and his discovery that the earth is not the center of the universe. Strangely, orthodox science and orthodox religion both are repeating a milder version of the cycle on an issue of equal importance - by not studying and seriously exploring the very considerable evidence for a life after the death of the physical body. This includes the research on reincarnation. Strange as it may be, we find that, like Galileo's findings, these reincarnation findings also stand up to scrutiny as observations of phenomena that are not necessarily replicable.

Reincarnation is one form in which hundreds of millions of people have conceived of the idea of life after the death of the physical body. Most major polls, including the Gallup, show that about 25% of people in the United States say they believe in reincarnation. There are many different kinds of reincarnation beliefs, but generally it consists of the notion that there is an essence, or spiritual identity, that cycles through various physical bodies through time. Different cultures have different versions, and reincarnation ideas have influenced, and been influenced by, the major world religions, especially Hinduism and Buddhism in India and China. In Western literature, reincarnation has been explored by Jack London, E.P. Oppenheimer, A.C.Doyle, and Johann Goethe, among others.

There are many very good texts exploring reincarnation in detail. Few people who study these cases will come away without appreciating the importance of this research. In this chapter, we will look at case studies in four major areas touching on reincarnation:

1. Spontaneous past life regression. In these events, ordinary people have spontaneous "memories," that later on match in some of their detail events that occurred months or years earlier.

2. Hypnotic past life therapy. This involves an intentional use of hypnosis, usually by a professional psychologist or psychiatrist, with a stated effort to recover "Memories" that might in some way help the patient recover frm symptoms or trauma presumably related to a "Past Life."

3. Children's reincarnation memories. Children will sometimes spontaneously recount events they claim happened in "another life." When investigated, some of these reports have been found to be accurate, with no known normal ways in which the children could have received the information.

4. The new research on birthmarks and reincarnation. Ian Stevenson has collected and analyzed a volume of cases, and offered photographs, in which the children's already investigated past life memories match through birthmarks the reported mode of death.

SPONTANEOUS PAST LIFE REGRESSTIONS: THE LENZ EFFECT

1. "IT HAPPENED WHEN I WAS JUST SEVENTEEN."

Frederick Lenz has collected a number of reports of spontaneous past life events, which have been called "The Lenz Effect." Jane was a high school student in San Diego. She was at home, babysitting for her little sister, and in the kitchen cooking dinner, when she heard a loud ringing sound in her head. Becoming frightened as it got louder and louder, she noticed that the sound came not from outside of her, but "...from within."

She thought she would pass out, as the room began to shift and fade, and suddenly she was on a cliff, looking out to sea. She does not say she *felt like* she was on a cliff, but that she *was* on a cliff. She watched the waves break and pound on the rocks below, and she could hear the sound and smell the salt air. She felt warm and happy in the sunlight, and was going back to her flock of sheep that she had left in the pasture. Singing a favorite song, she walked to the top of the hill, and thought of the Greek towns she would like to someday visit. Then sitting down near the sheep, she sang and rocked, all alone. "Then the vision ended, and I was back in my kitchen."

Jane was confused about what had happened, and considered it a vivid daydream. But then, a few years later, on vacation from college, she visited several European countries. One of them was Greece. She was attracted to some of the small coastal cities, and one day, on trip with friends, she came to a stretch of road that overlooked the sea. "I was filled with a number of conflicting emotions..." she said, and wanted badly to get out of the car. The driver pulled over, and Jane got out and walked to the edge of the road overlooking the sea. Then she must have been astounded to see the exact scene she had observed several years before in her parents' kitchen. She turned and walked away from the car, she says "...with a purpose, as if I knew the way." Following a path and ascending an embankment, Jane recognized the exact spot where she had been with the sheep. "It was exactly as I had remembered it. I was filled with memories of places and scenes, and I knew I had returned 'home' again," she said. Though it made no sense, at least to Jane, she felt that she had lived there, in another time. Trying to explain what had happened to her, Jane reports that her friends did not understand, so she gave up trying to explain the experience.[1]

It happened when I was just seventeen.

2. "I AM NO LONGER AS AFRAID AS I WAS."

Another Lenz case involved an owner of a foreign-car garage in Jacksonville, Florida. Always afraid of water, this gentleman had avoided swimming and boating, but after this dream remembrance, we might say he had a loosened spirit; he overcame his fear.

He dreamed he was on a boat headed out to sea. It was a small, well-worn boat, and he had left his home and headed down the coast, as he said, "...to trade with the savages." The weather was fair, and hot, and he enjoyed the feeling of the breeze striking his face. But on the third day out, the weather changed, and the storm at sea became violent, with heavy rain, huge waves. It must have been horrifying as the boat was "...whipped back and forth like a toy." There was a terrible sound as the boat smashed into something, and when he tried to swim, his legs got tangled in a line and he drowned as he was pulled under the boat. Always afraid of the sea and boats, he says, "My dream showed me why. I can understand my fear of the water now, and I am no longer as afraid as I was." [2]

3. A FRENCH-SPEAKING CHILD

In a number of his cases, Lenz had found that dreams of apparent past life events are far more vivid and memorable than ordinary dreams. But this is an account of a child, who had no exposure to the French language, speaking recognizable French, in a dream.

Roger and Lynn lived in Evanston, Illinois, in a modern housing development. One night they were aroused by strange sounds coming from their daughter's bedroom, but when they checked on her, they found her sleeping. They must have been shocked as she began to speak rapidly, in French, in an unfamiliar voice. Roger and Lynn say that their daughter was six at the time, had never been outside the country, and had never been exposed to a French-speaking person. Quite persistent, the child spoke French for several nights in a row, and her parents, having only had elementary courses in French in college, had trouble understanding what was being said. But shrewdly, Roger borrowed a tape recorder and recorded one of her conversations, then took the recording to a French teacher at the local high school. The teacher told them a heartrending story: the girl on the tape sounded distressed, and lost, and looking for her mother, from whom she had been separated when her village was attacked by the Germans. Roger and Lynn believe that their daughter had lived before, as a French child, and had probably died in one of the world wars. [3] Of course, there may be other theories to try to explain these strange events. But to be convincing, they would need to fit more of the facts than the reincarnation theory.

4. "MY EAR HURTS!"

Carol Bowman relates another story of a spontaneous past life regression which became therapeutic as events unfolded. Three-year old Blake was standing near a door watching his older brother as he waited outside for the school bus. Suddenly, Blake shouted, "Get out of the street! The bus is coming!" Colleen, Blake's mother, rushed to the door to see that Trevor was all right, and Blake put his hand to his head and said, "My ear hurts."

When Colleen asked why his ear hurt, Blake said, "A truck hit me." Not surprisingly, Colleen thought he had been hit by a toy truck, maybe thrown by his brother. But when she questioned him further, Blake insisted that it had been a *big* truck. Colleen apparently is quite sophisticated, and began asking carefully open-ended questions. Blake told her that he had been hurt in the street, that he had gone under the wheels of a big truck, and that he had been taken to a school. Wondering if this might be a past life memory, Colleen thought perhaps the school referred to a hospital, and asked Blake where his mother and father were when this happened. He said, "Gone bye-bye at the store." Colleen then asked Blake if he had died, and he simply answered, "Yes."

About a week later, without being asked about it, Blake told his mother that he had been hit by a truck like the garbage truck that was passing the house. Then, according to Colleen, Blake gradually became depressed, and seemed angry with his parents. He would say, "I love you and I hate you." Sentiments like this are not so uncommon, but we rarely hear them in one sentence. Apparently normally a happy boy, he had a neighborhood nickname of Smiley, so this behavior was not typical of him. With the depression he also complained of physical symptoms: a sore arm, a sore leg, always on the left side of his body. He called them "My ouches." Then Blake developed the frightening habit of wanting to run in front of trucks so that he could be run over.

Somewhere in this process, Colleen wisely discussed Blake's behavior with a therapist who gave suggestions on how best to approach Blake and his strange story. So again, Colleen asked Blake about being hit by a truck. Then she told him that he had been hit by a truck in a different life than this one, when he had a different mommy and daddy, and a different body. Apparently this was the right approach, since, according to Colleen, Blake's face lit up. She told him how much he was loved and cared for by everyone in the family, and according to Colleen, the depression and physical symptoms lifted almost immediately. Blake once again became his happy little boy self. Bowman believes that Blake was confusing his past-life parents, who had not protected him, with his current parents, hence his statement, "I love you and I hate you." [4]

HYPNOTIC PAST LIFE THERAPY

Modern interest in hypnotic regression got a strong push with Morey Bernstein's experiments, later written up as the Bridey Murphy case in 1956. Virginia Tighe, the wife of a Colorado businessman, was first hypnotized at a party by an untrained hypnotist, Morey Bernstein. She said that she remembered a life as an Irish woman, who was born in 1798 and died in 1864. Tighe said she had never been to Ireland, but gave details about ordinary daily life in Ireland of that time. Some of the details were accurate, but a Chicago newspaper published an article which said that Virginia Tighe had lived across the street from an Irish woman as a child in Chicago. That woman's name was Bridey Murphy Corkell. Tighe may subconsciously have learned details in that way. The case was, by some people, discredited, but for others, stands as strongly suggesting reincarnation. In any event, it became hot news in a culture that generally does not believe in reincarnation. Soon, Denys Kelsey, a psychiatrist, began making public use of past life therapy, and since that time, past life therapy has taken on new life, so to speak, in the work of hundreds, maybe thousands of therapists. Roger Woolger, Edith Fiore, Brian Weiss, and most recently, Carol Bowman have written public accounts of their work. These and other therapists are less interested in proving whether reincarnation happens than in treating their patients. In fact, some therapists even say that the patient's belief or disbelief in reincarnation has absolutely nothing to do with whether past life regression will help them to solve their problems.

Therapeutic results of past life therapy can be quite impressive and sometimes more dramatic than conventional forms of psychotherapy. Therapists have treated people for compulsive eating, phobias of all kinds, fluid retention, anxieties, sleep disorders, sexual difficulties, headaches and other pain, weaknesses, and death anxiety, among other problems. Some patients in hypnosis also have profound and healing spiritual experiences. There are thousands of such reported cases, and it is not reasonable to assign all such results to fraud, wishful thinking, creative imagining, or manipulation on the part of the therapist. Therapists and patients claim impressive results in terms of symptom remission, but few people claim that hypnotic regression memories "prove" reincarnation.

5. "I NEVER THOUGHT ONCE ABOUT THE CATS."

One of Woolger's cases involved a professional woman in her forties, who had a strange anxiety about leaving her cats alone in her city apartment. She must have been far more concerned than the cats, and had not been able to take vacations. In her earlier this-life experiences, there had been a few involving pets, but Woolger thought her anxiety was far out of proportion to the actual situation.

In hypnosis, she told a heartbreaking story. She was an old woman living in a bleak stone house. There was a storm, and she had been fighting with her husband, who said that she did not care about the children. The husband was outside the house screaming, and had the children there, and she would not let them in. This was a painful and risky situation by any standard. Then everything became quiet, and she heard a knocking. She believed her husband had sent their little boy to appeal to his mother, as had happened in the past, but rage kept her from thinking clearly. In the morning when the storm was over, they did not come back, so she assumed they had gone to an inn. She went to the door, but it would not open. When she pushed it, she found her daughter dead, on the threshold, and her son unconscious. Her husband was absent. She learned that he had tried to take the children to an inn, but had died of a heart attack. The children had come back, but she would not let them into the house. Eventually, the little boy also died. The woman had never told her neighbors, and had lived with the guilt for the rest of her life, never trusting herself to take care of anyone again, apparently including the cats.

Even Woolger himself must have been astonished, as he reports that at the end of the session his patient was greatly relieved and shortly afterward was able to take a two-week vacation, and had a wonderful time. She said, "I never thought once about the cats." (5)

6. "I'M VERY DISTRAUGHT."

One of Brian Weiss' cases involved a man whom Weiss says "...was plagued by an unreasonable fear of loss." In the hypnotic regression, Tom related slowly and in detail the circumstances of a life in England, where he described a troubled sense of "insecurity." He was a landowner, relatively well-to-do, and had two boys and a wife. Describing his surroundings as lush, with rolling hills and old trees, he lived in a country estate house, apparently quite comfortably. "I'm sort of established," he said, but the anxiety seemed related to his view that he was "...not in the upper classes," and felt that everything he had could be taken away from him, or that he could somehow lose it.

Tom moved to the next significant event, which was a fire in his barn. As he was trying to get the horses out, he saw that the house was on fire as well. His children were apparently away, but Tom said that his wife had died in the fire. In the hypnosis, Tom said that he thought the fire had been set by people in the village because he was Jewish. After the fire, he moved to America.

His last memory of that life was as an old man, on his deathbed, surrounded by his two sons and their families. He remembered a feeling of "...being injured for something I was, not for something I did." But he especially recalls the love from his sons, and the family feeling. "This was consolation for me," Tom said. Weiss does not say that Tom recovered from his insecurity as a result of the hypnotic regression, but seems to suggest it by saying that Tom learned the roots of his insecurity, along with the dangers of hate and prejudice.[6]

7. THE LYDIA JOHNSON CASE

This case was investigated by Ian Stevenson. In 1973, a Philadelphia doctor, Harold Johnson, was using hypnosis to help some of his patients, and discovered that Lydia, his wife, was an excellent hypnotic subject. While working with Lydia one day, he induced what appeared to be past life memories, and Lydia suddenly flinched and screamed, as though she had been struck. As she clutched at her head, the session was ended, but the headache would not go away. Repeating the procedure twice again, the results were the same. Lydia said that in the trance she had pictured a scene in which old people were being forced into water, as if to drown them. She felt herself being pulled down, and then felt a blow, then her headache. Johnson called in another hypnotist, and in one more regression, before the pain started, the associate told Lydia that she was ten years younger.

Immediately, according to the report, Lydia began to talk in broken English, and in a foreign language that nobody in the group could understand. She said she was a man, Jensen Jacoby, and began, in a mixture of English and Swedish, to describe a past life. It had occurred in 18th century Sweden, in a village. The session, and some following sessions, were tape recorded, and when Swedish linguists were brought in, they spoke to Lydia in 18th century Swedish and must have been stunned to find that she was able to understand and answer them, almost exclusively in Swedish. Jensen Jacoby reported, in Swedish, that he had been a farmer, and asked where he lived, he said, "in a house." He raised cows, horses, goats and chickens, and had built his own house out of stone. Apparently the Swedish linguists brought in a modern pair of pliers, and Jensen did not know how to use them, but identified an 18th century wooden container used for measuring grain, a bow and arrow, and poppy seeds.

This case, well established, is especially striking in that Lydia Johnson was not only able to speak the documented old foreign language, but also to respond when she heard it.[7] This is called responsive **xenoglossy** and there are other such cases.

8. "SOMEONE'S GOT A CLUB."

Edith Fiore, another hypnotherapist, gives rather long verbatim reports of her cases; we have summarized two of them here. One case involved a twenty year old woman whom Fiore calls Becky. She had suffered "terrible headaches" since she was thirteen years old, so severe that she would sometimes vomit and be sick for days. She also had the difficulty of not being able to experience sexual fullfillment. Fiore taught her self-hypnosis and gave her a tape to use for practice, and Becky was able to use finger signals to indicate answers from her unconscious mind. This is a simple but effective method that many therapists use to bypass the censoring conscious mind.

Becky began by describing a rather comfortable rural scene, with a young man, in England or Ireland. Then she spoke of her home and family, and eating "some kind of mush, white stuff." She described being abducted by a soldier on a horse, and kept with other women in a large stone building, apparently for sexual purposes. She felt used and resentful, but surprisingly said it "...was better than home" because it was "...more exciting." Later, she described an urban setting where she was walking alone, and was approached by three "angry looking" men. Becky became emotional as she described being dragged between two buildings. She said, "Someone's got a club or something – metal." She was hit twice on the head, and raped by all three men. The third man cut her with a knife, she felt somewhat detached from her body, "overhead slightly..." and believed that she had died. Becky made the staggering claim that one of the rapists had been her current father, but that she had forgiven him. Shortly after, it turned out that she did indeed have a deep and well-hidden hatred for her father, and a fear of his anger. The father came for one of the therapy sessions, and apparently accepted Becky's story since he wept and apologized for anything he had done to hurt Becky in a past life and vowed to do a better job of controlling his anger. The headaches rapidly decreased in both severity and frequency, her sexual problems decreased, and after several more sessions, with other memories, therapy ended. Becky reported two months later that there had been "No migraines! Not even one." [8]

9. "JUST LISTENING ...WATCHING"

Another of Fiore's cases involved Joe, who complained of severe insomnia, and said he depended on sleeping pills to get to sleep. Exhausted, he had trouble concentrating, and since he was studying for a real estate exam, his being upset about not concentrating and not remembering led to more anxiety. Of course this anxiety contributed to the sleep problems.

Over several sessions, Joe described events that happened as he, in another life, traveled west with a wagon train, heading for California. It was interesting that he said guns had always been important to him, and in his past life memories of the frontier, guns were of course needed for survival. He felt that he had been a good marksman, and relatively prepared for the trip west.

He then described the wagon train being attacked by Crow Indians. Apparently during that night he had killed two Indians with a knife, and stayed awake most of the night on watch before leaving to go it alone by moonlight at 3:00 a.m. Joe claimed not to have been afraid, but did describe hearing screams from time to time as someone was being attacked or killed. Joe developed quite a colorful career. He described robbing a stagecoach, fleeing to Mexico, then returning to California and being a guard in a drinking and gambling establishment. Later he became a sheriff, and found that role quite exciting. One night, playing pool with the banker and the mayor, Joe was shot in the stomach with a shotgun. Joe remembers his death, and being above his body. "It's like I'm looking through the roof." He also recalls having to be alert at night, always, because of the people who would like to have killed him, "...trying to make a name for themselves." Toward the end of the sessions, Joe said, "If all that was real, it sure explains my being so alert every night. Hope all that changes."

This whole story sounds rather bizarre, yet Fiore reports that Joe let her know weeks later that, following the last session, he had become able to go to sleep immediately and slept soundly through the night. He had no further need for medication.[9]

EVALUATION OF HYPNOTIC REGRESSION

Though many regressions are conducted by highly trained psychologists and psychiatrists, there apparently is a shortage of follow-up evaluation on cases like these to see whether the remissions have been long lasting. It is not hard to find such evaluations of cognitive therapy, brief therapy, marital therapy and family therapy, for example, but very hard to find evaluations of past life regression therapy, except by therapists describing their own cases. Presumably this is one reason why the American Psychological Association and the American Psychiatric Association do not officially encourage this kind of therapy.

One interesting exception is a study done in the Netherlands that showed that in about half the cases of Tourette's Syndrome treated with past life therapy, symptoms had largely disappeared and not returned after one year. (Tourette's Syndrome is a disease characterized by sudden, involuntary, jerky muscle movements and sometimes loud vocalizations.)

From personal experience as a therapist using hypnosis, though I did not encourage past life therapy, some clients under hypnosis would begin spontaneously to speak in convincing ways about previous lives. Sometimes their symptoms would decrease.

Although past life regressions are often dramatically effective, the respectability of past life therapy might increase if more quantitative studies on other kinds of cases could show that symptom remission is genuinely long lasting. Just as important, if lasting changes are demonstrated in follow-up studies, this would support findings below that suggest that reincarnation somehow is "objectively real."

CHILDHOOD MEMORIES OF PAST LIVES

The most important and convincing research on children's past lives, and of reincarnation in general, is the research done by Ian Stevenson. He is the former head of the Department of Psychiatry at the University of Virginia School of Medicine, and now director of the Division of Personality Studies at the same university. His works are long, detailed, and difficult to follow, even for professional researchers. One could say they read like professional detective stories for professional detectives. But for people in this field of study, he is the model for serious, honest, scientific work on reincarnation. His case studies cannot be surpassed anywhere for sheer detail, caution, and clear thinking. Skeptics may realize that these cases do not "prove" reincarnation, but if they are willing to do the work of reading Stevenson's own reports, they will discover that the evidence is really quite strong. Further, if reincarnation is established by the study of children's past life memories and of those memories that correspond to birthmarks, this would give a more solid theoretical basis for past life therapy as well.

10. "THAT'S THE OLD LADY. THAT'S ROSE."

One of Stevenson's cases occurred among the Tlingit Indian Tribe, which inhabits much of southeastern Alaska. With other tribes in the area, the Tlingits believe in reincarnation. Stevenson states that this tribe was one of the last to cross to Alaska from Asia, and so did not receive their reincarnation ideas from European sources. This tribe believes that souls reincarnate only among their relatives, so if a woman has a dream of a deceased relative, she expects that relative to reincarnate in her child. Especially if there are birthmarks similar to those of the deceased relative, the case is settled and the child will be given the name of the deceased relative.

Victor Vincent was a full-blooded Tlingit, and died in 1946. He felt especially close to a niece, Mrs. Corliss Chotkin, the daughter of his sister. On a visit, Victor said, apparently with great conviction, "I'm coming back as your next son. I hope I don't stutter then as much as I do now. Your son will have these scars." He showed the scar of an operation which he had on his back, with suture holes, and a scar from another operation on the right side of his nose.

Perhaps it was coincidental, but about eighteen months after the death of Victor Vincent, Mrs. Chotkin gave birth to a boy and named him Corliss Chotkin, Jr., after his father. And here the story becomes very interesting. This boy had two scar marks on his body in the same place and of the same shape as the scars of Victor Vincent, but for some reason, the discovery of the scars did not lead to the naming of the child after Victor Vincent. When his mother tried to get Corliss to say his name at thirteen months, he said impetuously, "I'm Kahkody." This was the tribal name for Victor Vincent, and the boy's statement led to his being given the name of Kahkody. At age two, while being wheeled along a street in Sitka in a stroller, he spontaneously recognized a step-daughter of Victor Vincent and called her by her correct name, excitedly saying, "There's my Susie." His mother had reportedly not yet seen Susie. Also at age two, Corliss recognized a son of Victor Vincent's and said, "There's William, my son." On another occasion, Corliss picked Victor Vincent's widow out of a crowd and said, "That's the old lady," and "There's Rose." Rose was her correct name and Victor had, according to Stevenson's information, always referred to her as "the old lady."

Corliss also narrated several episodes in the life of Victor Vincent, knowledge of which his mother was certain he could not have acquired through normal channels. One involved a fishing expedition during which his boat engine broke down. Victor Vincent put on a Salvation Army uniform (he was a part-time Salvation Army worker) and rowed a small boat to attract the attention of a passing ship. Mrs. Chotkin had heard this story when Victor Vincent was still alive, but was certain that her son had never heard it before he related it in accurate detail. On another occasion, on a visit to the home where Mrs. Chotkin had lived during the life of Victor Vincent, the boy pointed to a room and said, "When the old lady and I used to visit you, we slept in that bedroom there." The building had been remodeled and was no longer used for a residence and the room was not easily recognized as a bedroom. But Corliss was correct. There were a number of other correct statements made by Corliss, and several personality characteristics which he shared with Victor Vincent.

Stevenson reports that at about the age of nine, Corliss began to make fewer statements about a previous life, and by the age of fifteen, said he remembered nothing. This amnesia almost always happens in these cases as the child grows older.[10] This is a summary of a ten-page report by Stevenson.

11. THE CASE OF EMAD ELAWAR

A second case of Stevenson's occurred in Lebanon and was studied in the 1960s. It is a case from a Druse community, an Islamic group that has strong beliefs about reincarnation. The Druses believe that reincarnation happens immediately after death, but surprisingly are very slow to affirm that a particular suggestive case is really one of reincarnation. This kind of skepticism is useful in the research Stevenson has done. The first family interview occurred in 1964 when Imad was five years old. The information seems initially to have been given by the parents, based on things the child had said, rather than statements of the child himself. This might seem troubling, but the finding that the parents had assumed several aspects of Imad's story which proved not to be accurate assumptions, helped to validate the case in general. Also, this case is made stronger by the fact that the parents of the child claiming the memories, Imad Elawar, had not been in any contact with the family whom Imad said he had lived with. So Stevenson was able to interview the parents, the boy, and then go to the village of Khriby, twenty five miles distant, to interview the claimed original family of Imad Elawar. In all of these visits, Stevenson had another advantage: he worked with several interpreters so that he could compare the English renditions of the Arabic with one another.

Imad had at about two years old begun to refer to a previous life. As time went by, he mentioned many names from that life, some events, and several pieces of property he claimed to have owned. Thoughtfully, he often asked how these people were doing, and gave the name of the village (Khriby) and the name of the family with whom he had lived (Bouhamzy). Imad's father scolded him and called him a liar for telling such stories, but Imad, apparently convinced his memories were true, continued to talk to his mother. The father, apparently somewhat flexible, changed his position one day when a resident of Khriby came to Kornayel, the village where Imad lived, and Imad recognized him! According to Stevenson's report, even after this recognition, Imad's father and mother took no steps to verify that any of Imad's statements were accurate, but inadvertantly discovered that indeed Imad had correctly named villagers of Khriby. He had also named, in some of the first words he had spoken, "Jamileh" and "Mahmoud," and spoke of an accident in which a truck had run over a man, breaking both of his legs and causing other injuries that led to his death. He said he belonged to the Bouhamzy family of Khriby, and expressed a strange emotion: he was overjoyed that now he could walk. The parents assumed that he believed he was Mahmoud, and had been killed by being run over by a truck. Imad's father, Mohammed Elawar had never been to Khriby, nor had his uncle with whom he went.

When Stevenson first went to Khriby, he learned that a Said Bouhamzy had been killed when run over by a truck in 1943. A cousin of Said Bouhamzy was Ibrahim Bouhamzy, who lived near to the house of Said Bouhamzy.

Ibrahims's cousins, Haffez and Nibeh, were the principal sources of verification of Elam's story, and verified all of the following statements of Imad as being correct. As Imad had reported, there was a Mahmoud, who was an uncle of Ibrahim Bouhamzy. There was a Jamileh, known for her beauty, who was a mistress of Ibrahim. Jamileh dressed well and wore high heels, quite a remarkable thing in a Druse community. Further confirmed details were that Ibrahim had a brother named Amin who lived at Tripoli, Amin had a son named Telil or Talal, a brother named Said, a brother named Toufic, a son named Salim, a son named Kemal, and a sister called Huda.

In fact a truck had run over "a man" and he was taken to the hospital where he died a few hours later. It was verified that this happened to Said Bouhamzy. Also verified was that there was a bus accident involving Ibrahim Bouhamzy when Ibrahim was the driver, and several people were injured. Haffez and Nibeh also verified Imad's statements that Ibrahim and Said were friends of Kemal Joumblatt, a well-known Druse politician and philosopher, that Ibrahim was fond of hunting, owned a double barreled shotgun and a rifle, which he kept hidden as it was illegal. Ibraham had a brown dog, and had once beaten a dog. Ibrahim had a house in Khriby, near a slope, and there were two wells at the house. A new garden was being built at the time of his death, and Ibrahim had a yellow automobile, a bus, and a truck which he used for hauling rocks.

On the whole, though there were also a few inaccurate statements, Stevenson believes that Imad had accurate memories of events of which he could have had no normal knowledge. He believes that Imad's memories of a man being run over by a truck, his statement of how happy he was to be able to walk, and his notable phobia of large trucks and buses, which he reportedly showed even as an infant, were related. Imad also showed a number of Ibrahim's personality characteristics: he was temperamental, was intensely interested in hunting, was very precocious, and like Ibrahim showed a special interest and skill in speaking French, which no one else in the family could speak. The reader may have noted that there is some suggestion that Imad had fused some memories of Said and Ibrahim, but in questioning the parents more closely, Stevenson found that Imad had never claimed to be Mahmoud, and had never said that the fatal truck accident happened to him. There are other details and correlations, and this two-page description of the case summarizes a seventy-page case study written by Stevenson.[11]

Some readers will find these detailed "memories" of Imad, and of Victor Vincent, to be quite unbelievable. We can only say that very many people who carefully study this and other similar cases come away with changed beliefs about reincarnation.

12. THE BISHEN CHAND CASE

This case, another of Stevenson's, occurred in yet a third country, India. Bishen Chand Kapoor was born in Bareilly, India, in 1921. At the age of about one and a half years, he began to ask about a town named Pilibhit, about fifty miles away, where he wished to be taken, although nobody in his family knew anyone in Pilibhit.

He talked (endlessly, according to the record) of his life there, and by the time he was five and a half years old, claimed detailed memories of a previous life. His name, he said, was Laxmi Narain, and he had been the son of a wealthy landowner. He described the rather lavish house where he had lived, and said he had frequently enjoyed the singing and dancing of "nautch girls," who were professional dancers but also sometimes prostitutes. Quite a party person, he said he also went to parties at the home of Sander Lal, who owned a "house with a green gate." At one point, apparently impressed with his former lifestyle, Bishen precociously recommended to his father that the father should take on a mistress, in addition to his wife. Not one to take his fallen social position passively, Bishen Chand became resentful of the simple lifestyle of his latest family, and refused to eat the food, saying that in his previous life, even the servants would not eat such food. One day, Bishen's sister Kamla caught him drinking brandy, whereupon he announced that he was quite accustomed to drinking alcohol in his other life. Later, he said he took on a mistress named Padma, reportedly a prostitute, and claimed that he had once killed a man coming from her apartment.

This colorful story came to the attention of an attorney in Bareilly, K.K.N. Sahay, who went to the Kapoor home and recorded the outrageous things that Bishen Chand was saying. Later, he took Bishen Chand to Pilibhit, and discovered that a person named Laxmi Narain had indeed lived there, and died about eight years earlier. A crowd gathered and according to the report, nearly everyone had heard of the wealthy family with its "decadent" member Laxmi Narain, and remembered his involvement with the prostitute, Padma (who was still living there), and how Laxmi Narain had killed a rival lover of Padma's. Narain's family had been able to get the charges dropped, but Laxmi Narain, perhaps because of his lifestyle, died a few months later at the age of thirty two.

Taken to Laxmi's old school, Bishen Chand recognized some of Laxmi's old classmates in a photograph, one of whom happened to be in the crowd. Asked about their teacher, Bishen Chand correctly described him as a fat and bearded man. He also recognized the house of Sander Lal, which had the green gate. Neighbors verified that there had been singing and dancing in the courtyard and said that the name of the prostitute whom Laxmi had been associated with was indeed Padma. Apparently Padma was well known in the community.

When Bishen Chand met the mother of Laxmi, there was a surprisingly strong attachment rather immediately. He correctly answered her questions about his previous life, including one involving his throwing out of some pickles. Laxmi Narain's father was reputed to have gold hidden somewhere, but nobody knew where. Asked about the treasure, Bishen Chand was able to lead the way to a room in the family's former home. Later, gold coins were discovered in that room, but presumably it was too late for the family to make legal claim to them. Also, Bishen Chand's older brother reported that Bishen at a very young age could read Urdu words, though he could not have been taught them in his family. Laxmi Narain reportedly could speak Urdu. Bishen Chand also said that he preferred Laxmi's mother to his own.

This is an especially strong case, though not investigated personally by Stevenson himself. Early records were kept by an attorney, and many of the people involved in Laxmi's life were still living at the time of the investigation, including Padma. Nearly all the details Bishen Chand reported were verified, and, perhaps just as important, the likelihood of fraud is remote, since Bishen Chand's family had little to gain financially from association with Laxmi's family. It was well known that Laxmi's family had become destitute after his death.[12]

BIRTHMARKS AND REINCARNATION

Ian Stevenson has investigated a total of 895 cases of children who claim to remember a previous life. In recent years much of his work has involved an intense investigation of cases of apparent reincarnation accompanied by appropriate birthmarks. Stevenson has investigated 210 such cases, and found that among those children who claimed to have birthmarks related to past lives, 88% of the cases showed a correspondence in position or placement on the body, within 10 centimeters, between the memories of fatal injury in a past life with birthmarks in a present life. Also, by definition, these are often cases involving violent death.[13]

Other researchers have also studied birthmarks, and this is a hugely important line of study, tying as it does "spiritual" concerns and verbal reports with physically documented characteristics of patients.

13. A MURDER IN AGRA

We begin with a case from northern India, reported by Carol Bowman. It is fascinating and was documented and broadcast on BBC and published in the magazine, *Reincarnation International*. It was apparently not investigated with the care typical of Ian Stevenson, but nevertheless could be a genuine case of reincarnation accompanied by appropriate birthmarks.

At two and a half years, Titu Singh began telling of another life, in Agra in northern India. As he grew older he had specific memories which included being owner of a radio, TV and video shop, that his name was Suresh Verma, and that he had a wife Uma and two children. He said that he had been shot, then cremated, and his ashes thrown in the river. He said that he was homesick and wanted to go back to Agra, and even threatened to leave home.

Titu's older brother must have been interested in Titu's claims, and made a journey to Agra to check out his brother's story. He must have been surprised when he found a shop named Suresh Radio, and that it was run by a woman named Uma (Verma) whose husband had been shot. The brother approached Uma, who decided the next day to visit the Singh family and hear the story for herself. When the Verma family arrived, Titu was the first to spot them approaching, and recognizing them, shouting to his parents that his "other family" had arrived. He sat near to Uma, thoughtfully asked about the other children, and accurately recounted some details that only Uma could have known.

The families must have had some interest in establishing whether Titu's story was true. It was arranged for Titu to visit the home of Uma, and for Uma's children to be playing among other children. Titu recognized immediately which had been his siblings. He also correctly pointed out changes that had been made in the shop since Suresh's death.

Further, Uma corroborated Titu's story of how Suresh had been shot in the head while sitting in his car after arriving home from work. The autopsy report apparently confirmed that Suresh had been shot in the right temple, and that there was an exit wound on the left side of his head. When Titu's hair was shaven, the documentary showed birthmarks on each side of Titu's head. With more passage of time, Titu told the details of the murder to a court in Agra, it is said that he was able to "convince the authorities that he was in fact the reincarnation of the murder victim". Because of the police involvement, there is some independent documentation of Titu's story, and Suresh's parents are convinced that Titu is their dead son Suresh reincarnated. [14]

14. AN ENGLISH REINCARNATION CASE

This well documented case is that of Jennifer and Gillian Pollack. In 1957, The Pollack family suffered the deaths in an accident of eleven-year old

Joanna and six year old Jacqueline. When walking to Sunday mass they were struck by a crazed driver who erratically drove onto the sidewalk and mowed down the girls, both of whom died instantly. Their father, John, was a Roman Catholic who also believed in reincarnation, and prayed fervently that he would receive proof of reincarnation, and that in this way God would send his daughters back to live with him.

John's wife Florence became pregnant, and John became certain that his two daughters were returning to their family as twins. Florence's obstetrician maintained that there was only one child, but John insisted there were twins, and on the day of the birth in 1958 Florence gave birth to identical twin girls. They were named Jennifer and Gillian.

Immediately, the parents noticed that Jennifer, but not Gillian, had two birthmarks, and that they matched the size, shape and location of birthmarks which Jacqueline had had. One mark was a white line on Jennifer's forehead, and the other was a brown birthmark on her waist. According to Stevenson, identical twins have identical birthmarks since they have identical genetic material, so this was remarkable. Dr. Stevenson felt that the marks had been caused by something other than heredity.

When the girls began to talk, they described details about their deceased sisters which they had no normal way of knowing. When tested, they correctly identified toys that had belonged to their two deceased sisters, and when they returned to the town where the Pollacks had lived before the accident, they identified the house where the family had lived. They also on their own led the way to a park where their sisters had played, and described a school and swings even before they could see them. In a heartbreaking re-enactment of the accident, Florence heard them say, "Gillian was holding Jennifer's head and saying that blood was coming from her eyes because that's where the car hit her." Their father, John, believed that his prayers had been answered, and the Bowmans believe that this is a classic case of reincarnation, made stronger by the birthmarks.[15]

15. A GHASTLY MURDER IN KANAUJ

In 1951, six year old Ashok Kumar, nicknamed Munna, was enticed from play and brutally murdered by two neighbors with a knife and razor blade. The mutilated and severed head of the boy, with some of his clothes, were found, and identified by his father. Munna was the only son of Sri Jageshwar Prasad, a barber in the town of Kanauj, India. One of the murderers confessed, but retracted his confession when he was charged and learned that there were no witnesses to the crime. The case against the murderers collapsed and they were freed.

A few years later Sri Jageshwar Prasad heard that another boy in the same district, who had been born six months after Munna's death, had described himself as the son of Jageshwar, and had given details of his murder, named the murderers and the place of the crime, and gave other details about the life and death of Munna. This boy, named Ravi Shankar, (not the musician) felt entitled to have some toys which he claimed had been in the house where he had lived before, and kept asking his parents for them to be returned to him. Ravi Shankar's mother and older sister both testified that he had made such statements when he was between two and three years old. One of Ravi Shankar's school teachers when he was six years old reported hearing his story about the murder. Also, at the age of about four, Ravi Shankar gave an account of Munna's murder which corresponded closely with the account of the murderer who had retracted his confession.

Stevenson visited the site of the case, and had interviews with Professor B.L. Atrea, who earlier had collected written testimony from several witnesses, then also with Munna's father, with Sri Shriram Mishra, one of Munna's teachers, and with neighbors of Jageshwar Prasad. Details of these interviews are in Stevenson's report of the case.

Perhaps the most striking feature of the case is that Ravi Shankar's mother stated that when he was three or four months old she noticed a horizontal linear mark on his throat, and thought it to be congenital. As the boy grew older, he described the mark as a scar from the event of his murder. But by the time he was eighteen years old, and in college, he said he had completely forgotten the memories of a previous life. All he knew, apparently, was the general features of the case he had heard described by other people.

Stevenson was concerned about the fact that both families lived in the same general area, and that Ravi Shankar could have gained the information about the life of Munna through ordinary channels – neighborhood gossip, parental discussions, etc. Stevenson made every effort to expose such possible contacts, but after finding no evidence, was confident that this was a genuine case of reincarnation.[16]

16. A BAD DREAM IN TURKEY

Necip Unlutaskiran was born in Turkey in 1951. Before his birth, his mother had a dream in which she saw an unknown man showing himself to her with bleeding wounds. When Necip was born, he had seven birthmarks, some more prominent than others, and Stevenson first interviewed Necip when he was thirteen years old. When he was about six years old, he had begun to say that he had children and asked to be taken to them in Mersin, a town about 80 kilometers from his home of Adana. He said that his other name was also

Necip (a common name?) and that he had been stabbed. To simplify, we will refer to the first Necip as Necip the older, and the second Necip as Necip the younger. Necip the younger considered the birthmarks to be remnants of the stab wounds, and described the stabbing, but his parents paid little attention. Perhaps they were busy with other matters, as it appears they were more annoyed than interested. At age twelve, Necip the younger is said to have recognized his grandfather's second wife whom he had never met, saying that he recognized her from the previous life he claimed to have lived in Mersin. The grandfather's second wife had known a man in Mersin named Necip Budak and confirmed the accuracy of the boy's statements. Necip the younger also recognized several members of the family of Necip the older, who in turn confirmed the accuracy of his statements.

Apparently Necip the older had been a difficult and hot-tempered person, and often became drunk. He had been stabbed after injudiciously teasing an acquaintance, when both of them may have been drinking. Necip the older collapsed on the street and died the next day in the hospital.

Necip the younger said that he remembered, when he was Necip the older, stabbing his wife on the leg, and that after that she had a scar on her leg. Necip the older's widow admitted that this was true, and in a back room, showed several other women the scar. Also, Necip the younger showed considerable affection toward the children of Necip the older, and a jealous attachment to his wife. This may also have been difficult as he reportedly was so jealous that he wanted to tear up a photo of Necip the older's wife's second husband. In Stevenson's larger book, *Reincarnation and Biology: A Contribution to the Etiology of Birthmarks and Birth Defects,* he gives a summary of these birthmarks and shows their correspondence to the wounds which Necip the older recorded in the hospital where he died.[17]

17. SHE WORKED AT DUNKIN' DONUTS

In one of the few American cases, a woman who was a waitress at Dunkin' Donuts had a tragic experience with her first child. Her son had died at age three of invasive cancer. There had been a tumor in the right side of his head and another in his left eye, and one of his legs was also crippled. His mother was overwhelmed with grief, and the grief continued even after the births of her second and third children. But when her fourth child was born, he had birthmarks and defects that matched those of her first child: a nodule on his head at the site of the tumor, a defect in the left eye, and a defect in one leg that caused him to limp. There was also a seeping birthmark on his chest in the same position where doctors had inserted a feeding tube into the chest of her first son.

This case has more built-in weaknesses than other cases listed above: the mother's profound and lasting grief over the death of her first child creates a possibility that her interpretation of the events represents more wishful thinking than reality. The placement of the birthmarks could have been a coincidence which triggered her belief that her fourth child was her first child reincarnated. Also, her child apparently did not make statements about a previous life, and so no details could be independently verified. This case highlights some difficulties in reincarnation research, but the *possibility* of wishful thinking and coincidence, and the lack of child memories, do not necessarily rule out reincarnation in this case. They only make the case weaker.[18]

18. "BOY, WASN'T YOU MAD?"

Another American case was also investigated by Stevenson. The family did not want to be identified, and lived in a small house in the Blue Ridge Mountains of Virginia. The case involved a nine-year-old boy, Joseph

Boy wasn't you mad

(fictional name) whose family believed that he remembered the life of an uncle, David, who had died twenty years before the boy was born, when a tractor rolled over on him, crushing his chest. Apparently the accident did not cause external birthmarks, but may have created a medical condition:

Joseph had severe asthma, and as a result had missed quite a lot of school.

Joseph's aunt said that the family had been terribly upset over the accidental death, and had never spoken of it, so that Joseph could not have heard any details of his uncle's life. Stevenson recognizes that the possibility that Joseph could nevertheless have heard conversation does weaken the case. Yet apparently Joseph had offered enough details that he became the subject of Stevenson's investigation. For instance, he had always referred to his grandmother as "Mom," and called his mother by her given name, but this is a custom in some families. His mother, Jennifer, also reported an event when Joseph was staring at the roof of the house, and said, "Hey, Mom, do you remember when Papa and I got up there and painted that roof red for you and got it all over my feet and legs? Boy, wasn't you mad?" Indeed, David had once painted the roof and "got more paint on him than on the roof." The roof had been painted red in 1962, but apparently was later painted green, the color Joseph would have been seeing.

In another instance, Joseph and his mother were traveling on Route 11, and Joseph said, "When I was growing up, there was no houses here. There used to be all woods we went hunting in." He also said, "...that used to be a cornfield. I used to help pick corn with a guy named Garth Clark and Stanley Floyd." Joseph's mother did not know the men, but said, "...there's lots of folks named Clark and Floyd in this county." In fact, there is a Floyd County in Virginia. In another detail, Joseph's mother reported that as a little child, Joseph had always insisted that his new shoes had to be "...a ton too big for him. He'd say, 'Mom, you know what size I wear, a size eight.' It was a real pain. He wouldn't drop it." Apparently, David's shoe size was size eight, though the writer only implies it in a bit of literary drama.[19]

DISCUSSION

Because reincarnation is not as comfortable a concept in western cultures as it is in South Asia, Stevenson has, almost single-handedly, presented the most elaborate case studies in all of psychical research. Anyone reading them will be not only exhausted, but impressed with the effort Stevenson makes to rule out "normal" explanations for the information offered by the subjects, mostly children, about previous lives. Honest people will recognize that this research is not only serious but explosive: if Stevenson is right, it amounts to an earth-shaking contribution to the understanding of human nature. It also may help to validate the regressions observed in past life therapy, and in spontaneous cases. Stevenson's central argument is that the reincarnation theory fits the facts far better than any alternative theories. And what are these theories? Almeder has given a good summary of the theories, and his answers to them.[20]

HIDDEN MEMORIES This theory states that all so-called past life memories could have been gained by normal channels – parents, newspapers, lectures, radio broadcasts, TV, books, etc. The subject then forgets the information (perhaps because we are deluged with huge amounts of it) and spontaneously, or under hypnosis, remembers it. This theory may apply to some of the weaker cases, but really does not speak to cases such as Bishen Chand and Lydia Johnson. Bishen Chand knew where the gold was hidden, and if anyone had told him of it and known about it, we expect that person would have himself or herself found the gold. And who could have taught Lydia Johnson eighteenth century Swedish except a scholar of eighteenth century Swedish? Whenever subjects produce information that nobody then alive could have known, the *cryptomnesia* theory breaks down. (Cryptomnesia is the technical word parapsychologists use for this kind of event.)

GENETIC MEMORY This theory holds that everyone is born with specific genetic characteristics, and that memories are also coded in our genes. Emerging, they are misinterpreted as the subject's own memories. We do not know that such genetic memories do not exist, but in the richer cases it is possible to show that there is no genetic link between the subject and the person whose life is supposedly being remembered. It is known, for instance, that Bishen Chand was not in the blood line of Laxmi Narain, but it may be impossible to prove that Virginia Johnson was not of the bloodline of an eighteenth century Swedish farmer. On the other hand, in the Victor Vincent case and the Pollack case, there clearly were genetic connections. We might call this theory *genetomnesia.*

CREATIVE REMEMBERING This theory would explain cases in this way: in a culture disposed to believe in reincarnation, gullible parents interpret statements of a child as evidence of a past life. They may encourage the child to speak more, ask leading questions, then identify a deceased person whose life more or less fits the story they have created, go to that family and relate what their child has said. The grieving family uncritically accepts the statements as referring to the deceased family member, and not only is there some soothing of family grief, but on occasion there may be financial gain through publicity of the case. Researchers call this creative remembering *paramnesia.*

The objection deserves to be taken seriously, especially when there is contact between the two families involved before investigative interviews take place. In some cases there was this contact. In fact, Stevenson has presented some cases in which he says that, because of previous contact between the families, the cases may not be taken seriously. But in others, such as the Bishen Chand and Imad Elawar cases, written records of things the child said were made before there was any verification of those statements.

SLOPPY RESEARCH According to this theory, we should be skeptical of all reincarnation cases because researchers must depend on parents' and relatives' often poor memories and interpretations of things the child has said. Researchers also often must work through translators, so that language mistranslations are always possible. Answers to this theory are not hard to present: almost all historical research, including even the writing of textbooks, relies on the memories and interpretations of people in the distant past, and whenever non-English languages are used, misunderstanding is possible. Examples are too plentiful to list. Are we to discount historical research because of this? Also, in the best cases for reincarnation, these errors are unlikely: there is no large time gap between the beginning and the investigation of the case, no translation is involved, and many witnesses provide a check for the honesty and consistency of the stories. We can call this theory *hyperskepticism.*

FRAUD Some militant skeptics believe that Stevenson and other researchers may be themselves fraudulent, or if not they are naive by not recognizing fraud in the cases they examine. These skeptics usually have a hidden conviction that reincarnation simply cannot be possible, and some appear not to have read Stevenson's work. Yet there may be some validity in their concerns. Stevenson presumably has made money by publishing his books, and some families may have gained from the publicity that arose over the investigation of their cases. But anyone who reads Stevenson's painstaking work, and sees Stevenson's own concern about the possibility of fraud in some cases, will probably not take this theory very seriously. Moreover, many families are by no means anxious for publicity, and in fact tend to avoid it. In all of Stevenson's cases, a major focus is on corroborating reports by other people in the community. It is unlikely that fraud could not be detected if many other corroborating witnesses become involved in the case. Further, other researchers have replicated Stevenson's findings.[21] It is easy to suspect fraud, but unless there is fraud *actually detected* in these cases, we believe that the assumption of fraud arises more from the critic's prejudices than from the actual scientific evidence.

INFORMATION BY ESP This theory is based on the strong likelihood of the reality of extrasensory perception. Dr. J. B. Rhine, at Duke University in the second half of the Twentieth Century, and subsequently at other centers have exhaustively explored this phenomenon. It assumes that so-called "memories" produced by people who describe past lives are actually thoughts or sensations received by telepathy or clairvoyance from other people, living or dead, who had those experiences. According to this theory, subjects claiming reincarnation memories are actually subconsciously impersonating and dramatizing other people's memories. There are serious problems with this theory. First, the children do not show evidence of being particularly telepathic or clairvoyant in any other way. Second, telepathy or clairvoyance of the "voltage" that would be required in such cases is very rare, if it exists at all. Also, for large numbers of corroborating witnesses to support a child's report would require either massive fraud or massive psychic talent, and to explain children's memories in this way seems hopelessly complex and unreasonable. Finally, virtually nothing is known about the limits of ESP. This has been called the *super esp* theory.

BIRTHMARKS BY COINCIDENCE This theory says that birthmarks just happen to coincide with stories of violent death in children reporting past lives. Then parents, and perhaps even the child, unwittingly construct stories to fit the placement of the birthmark. For people in western societies, this theory might seem reasonable. However, in cultures where reincarnation is assumed, parents do not need to explore and explain birthmarks as related to a particular previous life. They are not happy if their children have birthmarks, but if there are marks, parents are usually content to simply say the mark comes from some previous life. Also, some deceased persons' lives are not exemplary, and parents, even in societies where reincarnation is a common belief, understandably are reluctant to encourage their child's identification with such people, or with lives either of extravagance or poverty. Moreover, Stevenson has done careful statistical studies on the placement of birthmarks, and of different kinds of marks. Statistical chances of the matching of memories, medical reports and birthmarks in many cases are in the range of millions to one. This theory is disastrously overused and can be called the *coincidence* theory.

MIND OVER MATTER This theory would hold that a mother, having knowledge of a deceased person's wounds, has the ability to impress a gestating embryo with certain birthmarks or other characteristics of that person. This assumes that the mother could modify the body of the child with her thoughts, then influence the child to describe a death matching the birthmarks she had created. This gives a great deal of power to mothers, and in the cases Stevenson examined in this regard, he could not find a motive for such behavior, even if it were possible. This theory can be called the *psychokinetic* theory.

RELIGIOUS AND THEOLOGICAL CONCERNS

In the Christian tradition, one New Testament passage has been the focus of considerable discussion regarding reincarnation. In Matthew 16:13-14, we read, "Now when Jesus came into the district of Caesarea Philippi, he asked his disciples, 'Who do people say the Son of Man is?' And they said, 'John the Baptist, but others Elijah, and still others Jeremiah or one of the prophets.'" Jesus did not argue with his disciples, but praised Peter when he said, "You are the Christ, the Son of the Living God." In this passage we can say that reincarnation is neither confirmed nor denied, and this ambiguity remains in Christian circles even to the present.

The percentage of Christian people in the U.S. believing in reincarnation is about the same as the percentage of the larger U.S. population believing in it. However, some church people have serious reservations about reincarnation, saying that it is un-Christian or even anti-Christian, or more charitably that it does not fit with Christian theology. More accurately, it does not fit with certain kinds of Christian theology or certain interpretations of the Biblical record. Theologians and Biblical scholars still are divided over whether one of the greatest of the early Christian theologians, Origen (185-254 AD.), and other early Christian leaders, taught the transmigration of souls or, not the same thing, reincarnation of a Christian sort. In the Second Council of Constantinople, in 553, the Church decided that such ideas minimize salvation, conflict with the resurrection of the body, are based on an unnatural separation between body and soul, are built on a too speculative use of scripture, and that the ideas are clearly false since no one remembers previous lives. Today, all but the first two of these judgments sound rather quaint, given progress in systematic observation of these phenomena. Origen was anathematized, probably more for political reasons than theological, and the later church relentlessly stamped out reincarnation in some of the darker chapters of religious violence. In the Twentieth Century, the Catholic Church has maintained that the gathering in which Origen and his ideas were condemned was not in fact an official church council. Through the centuries there have been serious theologians who believe that reincarnation is not antithetical to Christian faith, and that certain forms of reincarnation thought can be consistent with Christianity. Geddes MacGregor and John Hick have written extensively on the issue, along with other more conservative theologians.

SUMMARY

Over all, we believe that the case for reincarnation is not yet proven, but that it is impressive. This is one form in which people have conceived of life after death for millennia, and it is not likely that such a widespread belief could persist, in so many diverse cultures, without a strong foundation in actual human experience. If DNA testing can shed light on reincarnation, this might be seen in two ways in regard to life after death. On the one hand, the mutation of genes to create a second "copy" seems a wholly plausible and physical process, though random thus it does not have the same intrigue as NDE's for example, whose mechanism is not familiar. At the same time, even "mechanical" replication of a person through DNA matching is in any event a form of life after death. Perhaps not far in the future, DNA samples can be taken from children claiming past lives and compared to DNA samples from the deceased persons whom they claim to have been. If matches are found between people not related in families, this would seem to support reincarnation as the theory that fits more of the facts than any of the other theories listed above.

FOOTNOTES

1. Frederick Lenz, *Lifetimes: True Accounts of Reincarnation*, Bobbs Merrill Company, Inc., Indianapolis, IN, 1979, pages 27-28.
2. *Ibid.,* pages 36-37.
3. *Ibid.,* pages 37-38.
4. Carol Bowman and Steve Bowman, *Children's Past Lives,* Bantam Books, New York, 1997, pages 167-171.
5. Roger Woolger, *Other Lives, Other Selves,* Bantam New Age Books, New York, 1988, pages 96-97.
6. Brian Weiss, *Messages From the Masters,* Warner Books, New York, 2000, pages 101-103.
7. Cited by Robert Almeder, *Death and Personal Survival: The Evidence for Life After Death,* Roman & Littlefield , Publishers, Lanham, MD, 1992, pages 13-14.
8. Edith Fiore, *You have Been Here Before,* Coward, McCann and Geoghegan, New York, 1978, pages 26-54.
9. *Ibid.,* pages 171-189.
10. Ian Stevenson, *20 Cases Suggestive of Reincarnation*, University Press of Virginia,Charlottesville, VA,1974, pages 259-269.
11. *Ibid.,* pages 270-340.
12. Almeder, *Op. Cit.,* pages 5-8.
13. See http://www.childpastlives.org/birthmrk.ht, or Website Children's Past Lives Research Center.
14. See html://www.childpastlives.ort/titu.htm or Website Children's Past Lives Research Center.
15. Cited by Carol Bowman and Steve Bowman, *Op. Cit.,* pages 330-331.
16. Stevenson, *Op. Cit.,* 91-105.
17. Ian Stevenson, *Where Reincarnation and Biology Intersect,* Praeger, Westport, CT, 1997, pages 48-49.
18. Tom Schroder, *Old Souls,* Simon and Schuster, New York, 1999, pages 219-220
19. *Ibid.,* pages 220-222.

20. Almeder, *Op Cit.,* pages 25-58.

21. Antonia Mills, Erlendur Haraldsson, and H. H. Jurgen Keil, "Replication Studies of Cases Suggestive of Reincarnation by Three Independent Investigators," in *Journal of the American Society for Psychical Research,* July, 1994, Volume 88, Number 3, pages 207-219.

CHAPTER EIGHT

AFTER DEATH COMMUNICATIONS

"It (psychical research) is a field in which the sources of deception are extremely numerous. But I believe that there is no source of deception in the investigation of nature which can compare with a fixed belief that certain kinds of phenomena are impossible."

William James, M.D.
(1842-1910)
Philosopher and Physician,
Harvard University

Skeptics and believers in psychic phenomena have both emotional and rational arguments. Often the arguments are about whether or not "there is anything to it," and about the integrity, or lack of it, among people who claim to be psychics. Given the popularity of the topic, with dozens of new books by people such as John Edward, and James Van Praagh, and the portrayals of psychics on television and in movies like "Ghost" and "Dragonfly," one might think that the matter is settled: the dead communicate all the time. On the other side, with the blustering of the Scientific Committee for the Investigation of the Paranormal about the lack of serious scientific research in parapsychology, we might believe that all psychical researchers have been proven to be frauds and charlatans, and that the only thing worth investigating is the chicanery itself.[1] I believe that there indeed is a great deal of smoke and mirrors, but behind that smoke is a brightly burning and well stoked fire.

In this last chapter, we will try to make some sense of this topic about which there has been so much ado. There are three areas of exploration:

1. Early systematic research with mediums.
2. Modern studies of mediums.
3. Direct, spontaneous after death communications not involving psychics or mediums.

In the first two areas, I will present cases that have been *investigated* by qualified researchers. The last section consists of cases that have been *collected* by researchers who then look at the common patterns that are repeated in large numbers of cases. Both are valid means of exploration, and have been used in other branches of science, such as obstetrics.

EARLY RESEARCH ON MEDIUMSHIP

Early investigations of mediums were done by psychical researchers of the British Society for Psychical Research and its sister, the American Society for Psychical Research. These are interesting older cases. But as we as pointed out in earlier chapters, when these older cases have been investigated by skilled and cautious academic researchers, there has been good opportunity to weed out weak cases or to discover fraud. These cases are far stronger than modern uninvestigated cases. The early researchers went to great lengths to insure that the medium had no normal knowledge of the life or circumstances of the persons for whom readings were made. But with the experiments at Duke University, in which Dr. J.B. Rhine used card "guessing" and statistics to demonstrate the existence of telepathy, researchers gradually became more concerned about "Super ESP." Though only a hypothesis, it raised the possibility that mediums can "pluck" information from the minds of the sitters, then dramatize it as coming from the deceased. The reader will see in these cases that fraud and "Super ESP" are most unlikely, but cannot definitely be ruled out.

1. UNCLE JERRY

Oliver Lodge (1851-1940) was a well known English physicist who made original discoveries about lightning, electricity, radio waves and transmission. Deeply interested in psychical research, he worked, along with other S.P.R. researchers, with the Boston medium, Mrs. Piper. His summary of one sitting with Mrs. Piper follows:

"It happens that an uncle of mine in London (Uncle Robert), now quite an old man, had a twin brother who died some twenty or more years ago. I interested him generally in the subject, and wrote to ask if he would lend me some relic of his brother. By morning post on a certain day I received a curious old gold watch, which his brother had worn...I handed it to Mrs. Piper when (she was) in a state of trance."

Lodge was told almost immediately that it belonged to one of his uncles. Then, "...After some difficulty...Dr. Phinuit (Mrs. Piper's "control") caught the name of Jerry...and said... 'This is my watch, and Robert is my brother, and I am here. Uncle Jerry, my watch.'...I pointed out to him that to make Uncle Robert aware of his presence it would be well to recall trivial details of their boyhood..."

Then, Lodge said, "'Uncle Jerry' recalled episodes such as swimming the creek when they were boys together, and running some risk of getting drowned; killing a cat in Smith's field; the possession of a small rifle, and of a long peculiar skin, like a snake-skin, which he thought was now in the possession of Uncle Robert."

"All these facts have been more or less completely verified. But the interesting thing is that his twin brother, from whom I got the watch, and with whom I was thus in a sort of communication, could not remember them all."

"He recollected something about swimming the creek, though he himself had merely looked on. He had a distinct recollection of having had the snake-skin, and of a box in which it was kept, though he does not know where it is now. But he altogether denied killing the cat, and could not recall Smith's field." This must have been disappointing, but Lodge goes on.

"His memory, however, is decidedly failing him, and he was good enough to write to another brother, Frank, living in Cornwall, an old sea captain, and ask if he had any better remembrance of certain facts – of course not giving any inexplicable reason for asking. The result of this enquiry was triumphantly to vindicate the existence of Smith's field..., and the killing of a cat by another brother was also recollected; while of the swimming of the creek, near a mill-race, full details were given, Frank and Jerry being the heroes of that foolhardy episode." [2]

2. "HE RECOGNIZED EVERYONE BUT MISS WARNER"

This may be the most famous and most closely investigated mediumship case in over one hundred years of research. In 1888 a young professional man who used a false name of George Pelham, visited Mrs. Piper. She did not know who he was. Four years later, a month after his death, communications alleged to be from Pelham began to be received through Mrs. Piper. These messages continued for at least six years, and in sittings involving 150 different sitters (clients of Mrs. Piper), it seemed that the spirit of "Pelham" was communicating. From among these 150 people, "Pelham" recognized 30 whom he had known while living, and never claimed acquaintance with a sitter whom he had not previously known. This network of friends and associates was reportedly recreated and described with dramatic realism, and the deceased "Pelham" behaved in the sessions like a continuous, living personality. In other words, "Pelham" behaved, over time, as if he were still alive. It seems impossible that Mrs. Piper could have created such an accurate story line as to be convincing to so many people whom she did not even know.

Even one of "Pelham's" mistakes made sense. He failed to recognize, in one of Mrs. Piper's sessions, a young woman whom had met him before, named Miss Warner. In fact, Miss Warner had been only a child when "Pelham" was alive, and had changed greatly, so that he did not recognize her. This single event offers evidence that "Pelham" was more than some kind of construction in Mrs. Piper's mind. If he were a fantasy creation in the medium's mind, we would think that she would not have made such a "mistake."[3]

3. MR. EVANGELIDES AND THE CATHOLIC MEDIUM

A French journal on psychic research, *Annales des Sciences Psychiqes*, reported in 1905 a case in which a medium spoke while in trance a language completely unknown to her. Such cases are not so unusual. Judge John Edmonds, a highly esteemed and well-known judge of the Supreme Court of New York, had a daughter named Laura. At one time Edmonds had begun to study psychical research to show the foolishness of it all, but, as happens in many families, his fervently Catholic daughter embarked in a direction the precise opposite of her father's and became a psychic. Laura knew English and French, but we may imagine Judge Edmonds' chagrin when she suddenly began speaking Greek.

One evening, a Greek man named Mr. Evangelides visited the Edmonds, and later in the evening, Laura went into trance. Like Mrs. Piper, Laura also had a "control," a presumed deceased person who acted as a go-between to the spiritual world. This "control," named Mr. Botzaris, spoke Greek through Laura, and informed Mr. Evangelides about his son in Greece. Mr. Evangelides assumed that his son was alive and well, but Botzaris informed him that his son had recently died. The death was later confirmed.

Judge Edmonds had a change of heart, and submitted the following affidavit: "To deny the fact is impossible, it was too well-known; I could as well deny the light of the sun; nor could I think it an illusion, for it is in no way different from any other reality. It took place before ten educated and intelligent persons. We had never seen Mr. Evangelides before; he was introduced by a friend that same evening. How could Laura tell him of his son? How could she understand and speak Greek which she had never previously heard?" [4]

4. AN OBSSESSION WITH BEETLES?

Another of the great mediums studied by the British and American Societies for Psychical Research was Mrs. Gladys Osborne Leonard (1882-1968). In the Leonard "book tests" a deceased person would give a message to Mrs. Leonard of the page number in a book, the book's numbered position on a particular shelf of a library, in a particular house, which the medium has never visited. Then the sitter would find on that page of that book on that shelf in that house a passage which was related to past communications during the life of the deceased person. In most of these book tests the book, its location and the specific passage were not known even to the sitter, and certainly not known to the medium. Such cases argue against one skeptical theory about mediumship – that the medium is simply picking up information from the mind of the sitter.

Edward Wyndham Tennant, nicknamed "Bim" was killed in France in 1916. This sitting with Mrs. Leonard was held in 1917, and a message came that "Bim now wants to send a message to his Father. This book is particularly for his father; underline that, he says. It is the ninth book on the third shelf counting from left to right in the bookcase on the right of the door in the drawing-room as you enter; take the title, and look at page 37." Then the witnesses, apparently "Bim's" brothers or cousins, went to the house, and later wrote, "We found the ninth book indicated on the shelf was *Trees, ...* and on page 36, quite at the bottom of the page leading on to page 37, we read: *Sometimes you will see curious marks in the wood; these are caused by a tunneling beetle, very injurious to the trees...*" Signed: Glenconner and David Tennant. Unfortunately, in this description of the case, we are not told whether "Bim's" father was present in the sitting.

As it turned out, Bim's father was intensely interested in forestry, and his obsession with beetles had been a family joke. So the message was both humorous and appropriate.[5]

MODERN RESEARCH WITH MEDIUMS

Cases such as those above suggest that mediums need not "pick" information from the minds of the sitters and then present it as though its comes from the deceased. Also, strong precautions were taken to insure that the mediums had no normal knowledge of the information they were presenting. The early researchers were very sophisticated.

There are continuing modern research projects involving mediumship. One person exploring mediumship is Gary Schwartz, Ph.D. of the University of Arizona. At some risk of ridicule and the credibility of his career, Schwartz has been doing laboratory studies of mediums for about ten years. In the preface of his 2002 book, *The Afterlife Experiments*, he says, "This book is written for people who long to find scientific research on what they hold most dear – that love matters, that love evolves, and that love continues forever. Discovering the existence of the living soul may be one of humankind's greatest gifts. All of this is documented here for the first time." [6]

Mediums have been studied in other laboratory settings, such as the Consciousness Research Laboratory, earlier in Las Vegas, NV, and now in northern California, and at Duke University. However, Schwartz's work is interesting and provides an example of how such research can be conducted. It is not immune from criticism, but Schwartz does try to rule out some of the concerns that have plagued research on life after death for decades.

Schwartz wanted to know whether a psychic can receive accurate readings for sitters, and he wanted to answer the challenges of skeptics who say that without double-blind studies it is impossible to rule out very subtle messages being passed, even inadvertently, between sitters and psychics. Schwartz was able to gain participation from psychics Laurie Campbell, George Anderson, Rev. Anne Gehman, and George Dalzell. Following is a report on a small piece of a large study.

5. A 65% SUCCESS RATE

The psychic was Laurie Campbell. There were six sitters, one of whom was George Dalzell who also worked in other settings as a psychic. Laurie was not told who the six sitters would be, and contact with the sitters was only by phone, with the psychic's phone muted so that there was no input from the sitters. The sitters also could not hear the psychic. (Phone contact apparently only means that a call was placed, then muted for both caller and receiver.) The experimenters did not know the order in which the sitters would be on the phone with the psychic. Laurie Campbell's readings were tape recorded and transcribed and each sitter was sent two manuscripts, one of his or her own reading, the other a "placebo" which belonged to another of the sitters. The transcripts of course did not have the names of the sitter attached, and sitters were asked to determine which transcript was theirs.

Only the results for one of the sitters are reported in this small part of the study. Laurie Campbell's statements were 65% correct for George Dalzell and he easily selected which transcript was from his reading. He believed that only 17% of Laurie Campbell's statements were incorrect. Presumably, 18% of the statements were indeterminate. This is striking, and is an illustration of the use of careful isolation of mediums from sitters and a double-blind procedure. [7]

6. 77% AND 83 % SUCCESS RATES

In another of Schwartz's studies, two sitters, each of whom had suffered six or more losses of loved ones, filled out questionnaires about their losses, then several or all of the five mediums met individually with each sitter. Of course, the mediums did not see the questionnaires. There was no communication between the mediums about the sessions, and in each sitting the medium and the sitter sat in chairs separated by a screen. Sitter and medium were allowed to greet each other, and the responses of the sitter were limited to simple "yes" and "no" answers as to whether the medium was correct. The sessions were videotaped and verbatim transcripts were printed. The first sitter met with five mediums, and the second sitter met with two. An elaborate scale was devised to measure the accuracy of the mediums' statements.

Of the total statements made by the mediums, the average accuracy of the mediums for sitter #1 was 83%, and for sitter #2 the accuracy was 77%. Since this was a double blind study, there was a control group. The control group of college students found that only 36% of the mediums' statements would have been true for them.[8]

Though these studies can be and have been criticized, for open-minded people such studies and results are encouraging. They show that modern research methods can be used even to study such a difficult topic as mediumship.[9]

GUIDELINES FOR THOSE WHO WISH TO VISIT PSYCHICS

1. Read books on modern psychics, such as those by James Van Praagh or John Edward.
2. Avoid high priced psychics, be aware of how the psychic earns a living, and beware of psychics who ask you to return. Some may even offer to "remove a curse,' or say they feel "bad vibes" which must be removed for a fee.
3. Be moderately skeptical. Authentic psychics will want only yes or no answers from you, and will welcome questions. "Messages" from the "beyond" should be very specific.
4. Remember that psychics can be wrong on details, but you have a right to expect that most statements will be objectively accurate.
5. If you have a conversation with the psychic, make it after, not before, the reading.
6. Remember that older people who die naturally may be mentally and physically quite depleted. Because of this, they may take longer before they communicate than younger people who die suddenly. But the

younger people who die suddenly, on the other hand, may be more confused in their communications. This is documented by Robert Crookall in *The Supreme Adventure.*

7. Ask around for referrals to a good psychic just as you would for referrals to a physician.

DIRECT AND SPONTANEOUS AFTER DEATH COMMUNICATIONS

In this last section, we present a number of uninvestigated cases. In Case # Seven, because the psychic knew something of the circumstances of Mark's death, and because the things she said are not verifiable, they do not carry the weight of the cases mentioned above such as Oliver Lodge's work with Mrs. Piper, the George Pelham Case, or the book tests with Mrs. Leonard. However, **the fact that they are uninvestigated does not automatically invalidate them, but only makes them more open to question.**

Concerning after-death communications cases in general, they number in the thousands. Their sheer numbers, their spontaneity, and their logical consistency make it clear that something very important is happening. When we have large numbers of cases, we can see the patterns and a logical consistency among the varying details, so it is a different kind of research approach. In these cases we will see examples of sensing a presence, seeing a presence, hearing a presence, talking to the presence, touching the presence, the strange behavior of electrical gadgets, unusual behavior of animals, the conveying of feelings and specific information in apparently paranormal ways, and an encounter with one's holy mentor.

SEVEN OHIO CASES

7. WHAT IS IT LIKE TO DIE?

For several years after the death of my son, Mark, there were a number of informal sittings with friends who were also vessels for spirit communication. At the time I was doubtful that anything of value could happen, yet I continued the sittings, thanks to the kindness of J.J. and two other women. Though these sittings are not "investigated," and not validated in the manner of the cases above, the reports are fascinating. In view of the several validated psychic contacts surrounding Mark's death described in Chapter Two, and the dozens of other cases in other chapters, we can reasonably expect authenticity in these as well. Here are the most interesting passages from over fifty pages of records. The **content of the statements J.J. reported from Mark is consistent with reports we have seen in other chapters of**

this book, especially in the NDE: light, encounter with God, different sense of time, centrality of love, heightened awareness, confidence in life after death. Skeptics will of course say that the psychic is doing nothing but making up answers to the questions and saying things she believes to be true. We have seen earlier, especially in Chapters Four and Six, the danger of "nothing but" arguments. It is rarely so simple!

In a session on March 17, 1985, I asked Mark, "What it is like to die?" Mark answered, "Kind of scary at first. Remember bright lights, golden white. Visited with Great Spirit. Time has no meaning. Different Levels. Kindness, peace, love, happiness. No one misses earth plane. Can see all. Nothing like books. Died should not be a word. Passed on."

Then we asked other questions:

Question: Is there a Heaven or Hell?　　Answer: No.
Question: Describe it.　　　　　　　　　Answer: Earth is Hell.
Question: Is it being cleansed?　　　　　Answer: Yes.
Question: What is the next level?　　　　Answer: novice intern
Question: Are you studying?　　　　　　Answer: Yes.
Question: What are you studying?　　　　Answer: Wisdom, God.

March 31, 1985, Mark says, "Make the best of it. Learn everything. Top level must be a victory for all spirits."

April, 1985, Mark says, "Quarter is your evidence. Take it or leave it, Dad." (See "SOMETHING ABOUT A TREE" in Chapter Two.)

April, 1985, Mark says, "I love cop episodes. Have fun, unlike Hoover, like over. There is great love to be found. Get in the good times, Dad." (Mark may have thought J. Edgar Hoover, the cop, did not have much fun?)

8. I LOVE YOU, AND GET SOME MORE TREES

An Ohio woman, Deborah, describes several tender events in which she both saw and heard her husband. "About two years after my husband's death, I was sitting on the patio, and Bob came out of the pine trees and we walked across the yard together. Bob said, 'Everything is going to be OK, but get some more trees. They're going to build an industrial project next to you.' Then he told me that he loves me, and he was gone."

And on several occasions, when she felt confused, Deborah has said, "Oh Bob, I don't know what I'm doing!" "Then a blueprint comes," Deborah says, "like once Bob said about a leaky toilet bowl, 'Get a fishing weight and put on there.' " She did, and it worked!

In yet another event, Deborah says that her husband appeared in a circle at the bottom of her bed, but looked young, as he had when they were dating. He said, "I have things to do, and you need to get on with your life." Then, Deborah says, "I had a sort of question come into my thoughts, like 'What are you doing?' and he answered, with an empty smile, 'Studying the Universe.'"

9. A GREEN ROSE

Carla, a hairdresser living in Ohio, tells this story in which a most unlikely event suggests communication from her aunt to her mother. "My mother and my aunt had an agreement, that whichever one died first would bring a green rose to the one still living. Since neither of them had ever seen a green rose, they chose it because they wanted to pick something unusual. My aunt died first, and a friend of my mother's, who lived in Michigan, visited mother and brought her a green rose. The woman told her she had never seen a green rose, and thought my mother would like it."

10. RISING SUN

Carla also tells this story which suggests an unlikely communication between her mother and her great grandmother. "Once I took Mother to a psychic retreat center, and a psychic told her that she saw a rising sun, and it was somehow connected with Mother's grandfather. She also said that her grandfather had worked with Indians and that Indians worked with him. Mother didn't believe it, and only remembered Grandfather as being a security guard. When my mother asked her mother about it, she was told that when he was younger, her grandfather had lived in Rising Sun, Ohio, (an actual northwest Ohio town) and did in fact work with Indians in that area. My mother never knew that, and neither did I."

11. TREMBLING AT BEING SO CLOSE

A widow had this experience of touch: "About a month after Bill died, one morning at about 3 a.m. I felt a presence next to my bed, which sat on the side of the mattress! I could feel the weight on the mattress, and then I could feel it lie prone next to me and, and put its arms around me. I could feel the warmth, the trembling, at being so close. I reached out with my hand and placed it on the hugging arm, and patted it with wonderment and joy. It only lasted a moment, but it was real. How wonderful!"

12. SOMETHING LIKE A WATER BALLOON

An accountant named Jean had this experience of touch, combined with her neighbor's sense of touch and the ending of a troublesome "presence" in the house. "My old neighbor had a room which she kept closed off. It was a spare bedroom, and even when the door had not been opened, something would fold back the bedspread, and sometimes she would find the pillows at the foot of the bed under the sheet!"

"One day I went over and told my neighbor that if she would hold the door open, I would try to clear the house. There was nothing in the bedroom, or in the hall, but when I went into the bathroom, I bumped into something that felt like a water balloon. My neighbor was holding the door open and said she felt something moving at the door. It had been going on for nine months, but it never happened again after that." Jean and her neighbor have no idea what, or who, the energy might have represented.

13. IF WE WERE INDIANS, I'D SAY, "THERE GOES HER SPIRIT!"

M.W., an Ohio grandmother, tells of the death of her eighty-eight year old mother in October, 1993. "My brother, who lived with my mother, called in the morning and said, 'I can't get mother awake.' My husband and I went down immediately, as we lived just three houses away. My mother's body was still warm. All our four children were summoned. Grief-stricken, we were standing in the family room waiting for the mortician to come. My sons-in-law are hunters, and even my one daughter is a hunter, so this story

If we were Indians

is really strange. We live right on the Maumee River, and just as we stood there, a buck deer with huge antlers swam across the river (it's a big river) and stood in the yard looking up at the house. We've never had a deer do that, and he stood quietly for about twenty minutes. Deer just don't stand still in the open in mid-day! Then he walked right by the house and up the driveway. If we were Indians, I'd say, 'There goes her spirit!'"

M.W. describes in Chapter Three, #14 her own illness and NDE. After being in the hospital herself for a month, on Thanksgiving, M.W. desperately wanted to go to her mother's grave, feeling that she needed better closure on her mother's death. The doctor allowed her to leave for two hours from the hospital. Her husband took her to visit her mother's grave in a small local cemetery near the woods. To her joy and surprise, she said, "When I got to Mother's grave, it was all covered with deer hoof prints."

PUBLISHED COLLECTIONS OF DIRECT SPONTANEOUS AFTER-DEATH COMMUNICATIONS

There is increasing interest in spontaneous and direct but uninvestigated After Death Communications, and recent collections contain intriguing reports. We draw from several of them: The first is from Bill and Judy Guggenheim as it is published in their book, *Hello From Heaven*. The Guggenheims collected 3300 first hand accounts of After-Death Communications from about 2000 people, from all fifty states and the thirteen provinces of Canada. The second collection is that of Louis LaGrand, published in *After Death Communication: Final Farewells*. Other collections are those of G. Scott Sparrow, Celia Green and Charles McCreery, and Sylvia H. Wright.

14. HIS PLANT LOOKED REALLY RATTY

A thirty eight year old hairdresser in Florida sensed a presence: "One afternoon, I was watering plants on the porch. Fred and I loved plants – that was something we shared. As I was watering them, I came to one plant that meant a great deal to him. It was really looking ratty, and I wasn't crazy about it." Then she says, "As I was standing there thinking how badly the plant looked, I had this sensation Fred was right there with me. I felt him very strongly. I knew that Fred was behind me. I felt if I were to back up two steps, I would bump into him. It gave me a nice feeling, and I kind of laughed and went on." [10]

15. CLEAN UP THE HOUSE NOW!

A ninety year old writer and artist reported hearing a voice that gave him orders: "I have been contacted by my wife, Grace, many times. I have had long conversations with her. I ask her questions, and her words come into my head. For example, I was standing by the stove one day and felt her right beside me. I asked her, 'Do you have any advice?' And she said, 'Clean up the house now!' It was like an order." Grace must have been quite a strong-minded woman! Then he goes on: "So I said, 'O.K. I will.' I started picking things up, and just as I got through, the doorbell rang. Three of her Delta Kappa Gamma sorority sisters came to visit me. One was the president of the whole outfit! I know very well that Grace knew they were coming and gave me that warning. I was amazed when this happened." [11]

16. C .S. LEWIS: AUTHOR AND PROFESSOR

In *A Grief Observed*, the famous writer C.S. Lewis describes his crushing sense of loss and his sense of his wife's presence after her death. Even Lewis stumbles with forming his words.

"I said several notebooks ago, that even if I got what seemed like an assurance of H's presence, I wouldn't believe it. Easier said than done. Even now, though, I won't treat anything of that sort as evidence. It's the quality of last night's experience – not what it proves but what it was – that makes it worth putting down. It was quite incredibly unemotional. Just an impression of her mind momentarily facing my own. ...One didn't need emotion. The intimacy was complete – sharply bracing and restorative too – without it. Can the intimacy be love itself...? If so, how many preconceptions I must scrap! ...It would, if I had a glimpse be – well, I'm almost scared of the adjectives I'd have to use. Brisk? cheerful? keen? alert? intense? wide-awake? Above all, solid. Utterly reliable. Firm. There is no nonsense about the dead." [12]

17. J.B. PHILLIPS MEETS C. S. LEWIS

Phillips, who created the Phillips Translation of the New Testament, tells of a visual encounter with C.S. Lewis a few days after Lewis's death. Phillips did not know Lewis well, but in his vision the dead author appeared bringing a message that was related to a difficulty Phillips was having at the time. A week later, as Phillips read in bed before going to sleep, Lewis appeared again, even more alive, with the same message, but we are not told what the message was. [13]

18. OLD SPICE

An employment counselor had this joyful experience of her dead son's presence, in which she smelled a fragrance. "It was about eight months after Derek died, and I had just come home from shopping. As I unlocked the door to the house, I could smell Derek's aftershave. It was very strong. He used Old Spice, which has a very distinctive aroma – it was unmistakable! The fragrance was right in the doorway, like he was waiting for me." The mother must have been quite astonished, but somewhat skeptical as well: "I knew immediately that it was Derek. But just to make sure I wasn't hallucinating, I went into his room and opened a bottle of his Old Spice that I still had, and it was exactly the same smell! I also wanted to make sure that the bottle hadn't fallen or broken and that the lid was sealed, which it was. I couldn't see him, and I couldn't touch him, but I knew Derek was there. I had the strong sense that my son was sending me love." [14]

19. MY SCHOOL BOOKS DROPPED OUT OF MY HANDS

A granddaughter reported this event a month after her grandmother's death in which she both saw and heard her deceased grandmother. "One November afternoon I arrived home from school, and passing through the dining room I noticed my grandfather in his sitting room talking to my grandmother (who had been ill)." It all sounds very normal, and the granddaughter went on: "She was sitting on the couch brushing and combing her hair. She was in her nightgown and robe. I entered the room and said hello to them, and told my grandmother it was nice to see her feeling up to being out of bed. After a minute or two of polite conversation, I said I had better go do my homework. My grandmother then said, 'Barbara, it would be best if you don't tell anyone I was up and that you spoke with me.' I went upstairs and as I entered my own room it suddenly came over me that my grandmother was dead! She had died a month earlier. My school books dropped out of my hands." [15]

20. HE TOOK ON A VERY YOUTHFUL APPEARANCE

A woman employed by an economic development association gave this report of both seeing and hearing her deceased father. "Driving home from my mother's house, my father came before me in a vision three weeks after he had passed on. It was something I was seeing inside my head. At first he appeared the same age as when he died. Then he brightened up considerably and had a big grin on his face" The daughter must have been pleased and relieved, and went on, "As he began smiling, he took on a very youthful appearance. He was very healthy and very happy, glowing with peace. His whole communication seemed to be 'I'm all right. This is the way you should remember me.' Then I saw all my relatives that had passed over come around him, as though they were meeting him. They looked as they did when they were still alive. They were very healthy, very happy, and very loving. This experience gave me peace and made it easier to accept my father's death." [16]

21. YOU'VE GOT TO LET ME GO

A twenty one year old homemaker gave this report of feeling a presence and hearing the deceased. "Seven or eight months after my father died, I was still grieving very hard and really wasn't getting on with my life. I had a hard time accepting his loss and was drowning in my sorrow. This experience felt like a dream, but it was more like an alpha state. I felt my father's presence and heard him say, 'I want you to knock this off! I love you and I love your mother. But it's time for you to get on with your life. I'm happy now where I am. Please stop wishing me back. I've got other things to do. You've got to let me go.'" This was probably not what his daughter wanted to hear, but she goes on: "After that, I was very alert, very awake. I saw my father standing in the corner of my room. I could see him fairly clearly, from his head down to his waist. He had a look of contentment, like he wanted to show me that he was okay. I felt love from him, and then he was gone. This changed me almost instantly. I felt like a ten-ton weight lifted off of me. I felt such peace and acceptance about my father's death that I could then go on with my life and not continue in a downward spiral." [17]

22. ALL VERY HAPPY BEING DEAD

A dance teacher gave this report of both seeing and hearing, in a dream, several deceased people at once. "Then I had what was the strongest, most vivid dream of my life. All of a sudden I was transported to our old family home and then in comes my grandmother and in comes my mother and it was as real to me then as we are sitting here talking. And we hugged and kissed and laughed and giggled and we were just talking away and then I said, 'Wait, what are we doing here?' And I realized my mother had been dead for ten years." This is astonishing enough, but there is more: "I didn't think my grandmother was dead. Well, they smiled at me. We were sitting at the kitchen table, and they said, 'We don't want you to worry and we're all right. We're home, everything's fine and we'll see you again soon.' And then I woke up my partner and told him all about it and it was like two or three in the morning and I took note of the time. Next morning my dad woke us up with a call and he said, 'Grandma died last night,' and he said when she'd died and it was within minutes of the time that I had noted." [18]

23. HIS LAMP TURNED ITSELF ON AND FLASHED OFF

A college librarian reports strange behavior of electrical gadgets, and a suggestion that a blind person could see after the death of his physical body. (See also cases #23 and #31 in Chapter Six.) "The day after Paul's memorial service, while Keith and I were standing near Paul's lamp, it turned itself on. It had never done anything like that before. Our building was a sturdily built high rise erected some seventeen years earlier; it had no apparent defects in its wiring or electrical outlets." Then, according to her notes of the event, she says, "Keith 'turned off – he's sure – Paul's lamp, but it started flashing on and off, short flashes of light coming infrequently and seemingly in response to things we said. For instance, when Keith mentioned Paul's spirit visiting Paris (which Paul had adored and where he kept up with friends and former in-laws), after a couple of seconds the light blinked on for a flash, then went dark again.' Twice that evening his lamp turned itself on and flashed off and on in what seemed to us a highly meaningful way. We tried to ask it questions, urging it to flash once for yes and twice for no, but in this respect it didn't oblige. What it seemed to be communicating to us most of all was that now his spirit could perceive the difference between on and off, light and dark. In other words, he could see again." (*Paul had been totally blind from diabetes.*) [19]

24. THAT'S THE THIRD TIME – I DON'T LIKE IT

Two friends had been traveling, and both saw a presence, which was also seen by a stranger at the same time. "Some years ago, a friend and I were returning from an outlying village. It was a mild clear night with half-moon. Coming through an avenue of trees, we approached a large open field with

That' the third time, I don't like it.

houses on the opposite side of the road. *Appearing to float across that field,* just above ground level, was the figure of a woman with arms slightly outstretched. She was completely colorless, with the exception of her long fair hair which streamed behind her." This must have felt like Halloween! The young woman goes on: "We both stopped dead and watched. To our utter bewilderment, she disappeared straight through the wall of the convent school opposite. A man cycling towards us dismounted and inquired, 'Did you see that?' We replied we certainly had. He left us saying, 'That's the third time - I don't like it, I don't like it.' 'She' was gliding roughly one and a half feet above ground level." [20]

25. EVEN THE TURKEYS CAME TO THE FUNERAL

Here is another report of strange and unexpected behavior in animals. This one is given by a psychologist who was a pall bearer at the funeral of a friend. "For years before her death from cancer, Mrs. M. had lamented never having encountered a wild turkey despite her attempts to see one. She had lived in a rural area of northern New York, which had an abundant supply of the birds, yet they had eluded her grasp. When the funeral procession arrived at the cemetery and was proceeding to the grave site on foot, a whole flock of turkeys flew into the cemetery and stood a mere 100-150 feet away; not feeding, barely moving, just standing there for several minutes before moving off." [21]

26. SPECIFIC AND ACCURATE INFORMATION

A retired nurse sensed a presence, which also spoke to her. "Graham passed away when he was eighty-nine years old. I guess his heart just gave out. I had this experience with him before I knew he had died. I felt his presence in my kitchen. He said to me, 'Tell Vera,' who is my sister, 'to look real good around the desk in her living room. Take the drawers out and look in the back.' I wrote a letter to Vera and explained my experience to her." Vera must have been amazed, because later, when Vera's daughter called, "she told me they went through the desk and found about $3,000 in $50 bills he had hidden away! Obviously, Graham wanted Vera to find the money so it wouldn't be thrown out accidentally. All through his life his main interest seemed to be money, but I think he was more concerned about his wife's security." [22]

27. YOU ARE LOVED

There are reported encounters with religious figures in many religious traditions, and we saw several in Chapters Three, Four, and Six. This is a report of an unexpected contact with Jesus. "Then he came to me in an appearance that was sudden, intense and brief. I was in one of my depressions – one of my crying jags when I felt totally worthless and unloved, self-hating, and alone. In my black pit there was suddenly a window thrown open and love and light streamed down on me. I saw the Christ (in her mental version of what he would look like) and he said to me, 'You are loved.' It was there for one clear instant and then it was gone and I was reeling from it. The depth of my being felt changed and I have since felt an inner confidence in the love that is there and in the certainty of Christ's reality." [23]

DISCUSSION

When a loved one dies, all of us feel the pain of our own personal sense of loss. We also want some reassurance that our loved ones are all right, that we will see them again, and that life has meaning in spite of death.[24] And contrary to the opinions of Feuerbach (a 19th Century Bavarian philosopher, b. 1804, d. 1872, who was an articulate critic of nearly all religious ideas) and Freud, (the "Father of Psychoanalysis" b. 1856, d. 1939, who generally believed that religion is a result of neurosis) the fact that we *wish* for this reassurance does not invalidate the findings of the research.

Since these direct and spontaneous cases are not investigated, it is difficult to discuss their validity, though we may sense that many are completely valid. But the consistency of the cases, their frequency, and the emotional impact on those who encounter After-Death Communications, make them very important, and there is great deal we can learn from them.

For example, when we have these kinds of experiences, it is important to remember that they are not evidence of mental instability, or even of unresolved grief. They are normal occurrences, even gifts, and should be coveted rather than doubted and buried.

Moreover, people who do not believe in life after death are about as likely to have them as are those who do believe. Research has shown over and over that these kinds of events are not dependent on our belief systems.

Here is further advice: if you have an encounter, don't keep it hidden, but **share it** with a trusted family member, friend, or clergy person. You will find that these events are not so unusual. Also, pay attention to your deep emotions and thoughts about what has happened. It is not healthy to try to ignore or minimize them.

If you have not had an After Death Communication, don't conclude that it will never happen, or that your loved one does not care enough to communicate, or that you have been permanently abandoned. Be open and patient, especially if you grew up in a family that did not discuss or believe in such occurrences. We believe that our loved ones *wish* to communicate. Also, it may take deceased people some time to get their energy together and to "come through." Some events happen years or decades after the death occurs.

Be aware that strong emotions like bitterness, guilt, anger and fear can block our receptiveness to these experiences. It is best to try to resolve these feelings, though communications apparently can even occasionally happen in spite of them.

You may increase the likelihood of encounters like this by simply asking for a sign that your loved one is still alive and O.K. Or directly ask your loved one to communicate, if necessary during sleep in a dream, since that is the time we are less distracted and more relaxed. Visualize his or her face, or hear the sound of his or her voice. If you have a sense that your loved one is trying to communicate, or even if you don't, it can be helpful to sit quietly, breathe deeply, and try to clear your mind of unimportant details.

Anticipate that an After Death Communication will happen, but do not block it with your impatience. Sometimes these communications will give us information that helps us to deepen and enrich our lives, and to grow in spirituality. They often suggest that our loved ones go on learning, that there are jobs and ongoing projects in which they participate.

Look for social and spiritual support by joining a Bereavement Support Group. There are many such groups, and you will meet people who have had the same kinds of experiences described in this book. Don't be afraid of strong emotions or of becoming tearful – there will be other people just like you. You will be helped by other people's experiences, and in turn you will be able to offer help to them.

Internet Keywords "Bereavement Support Group" will produce titles of books on joining and leading such groups, and a Directory of Bereavement Support Groups and Services.

SUMMARY

My work with grieving people has shown me that the information in this book is extremely helpful. But this area of study has an even larger importance in the world we inhabit.

On the Outer Level, philosopher Neal Grossman has written a passionate and hopeful article, which we summarize here.[25] Our society is realizing that the evidence for life after death is growing more public and more persuasive. Signs of this are everywhere: books, professional journal articles, television and movies, and in more open personal conversations. It is an easy step for people to see that our real identity is not in our physical bodies, important as they are, but in our mind or consciousness, so that our lives can take on the luminous flavor of eternity. In another easy step, many people are realizing for the first time that if the findings of near death experience research are true, then we will experience our own life review, and our own judgment. From the findings of the research, rather than an eternal punishment in hell, whatever pain we have inflicted on others will be experienced as our own pain in the life review. The major world religions have all taught that the purpose of life is love and learning – to learn as much as possible about both this world and the transcendent world, and to grow in our ability to feel compassion and to act in loving ways.

Further studies will only increase the evidence that these things are true. Materialism, the belief that everything can be explained in physical terms, has already been shown to be false, and eventually there will be a major change of thinking in our culture as people "catch up" with modern scientific views. Scientists will begin to announce these and other findings, and it will become more and more difficult to sustain a culture built on greed, ambition, material possessions, wealth, reputation, social status, and a fear of death. Many people will be threatened by such change. But those who are convinced of an afterlife, and of the importance of love and learning, will become more committed and more vocal. They will have a stronger basis, built on both science and religious insight, for their efforts to transform and renew our planet.

On the Inner Level, psychiatrist Stavislav Grof[26] and others who work with non-ordinary states of consciousness have discovered that few people in western society experience the ecstatic sense of being reborn and of losing the fear of death. Yet well developed spiritual practices of meditation, drumming, chanting, certain forms of yoga, and prayer, as taught in Islam, Hinduism, Christianity, Judaism and Buddhism, and many tribal cultures will often trigger these experiences. Modern techniques of hypnosis and body work also will elicit such events, sometimes with paranormal components as well. So in addition to the implications for life after death, the fascination with **outer events like** NDEs, DBVs, OBEs, Apparitional Events, After Death Communications, is that they also sometimes elicit these ecstatic life-altering **inner** changes. So with this topic of Life After the Death of the Physical Body, we have a meeting point of **outer and inner experiences**, just as we have a meeting of **science and spirituality. However the events happen to us, ecstasy and the loss of fear of death offer an opportunity for a quality of life of which many of us in western culture have not even dreamed.**

Such events can lend to life the most exquisite brilliance, or as the 13th Century Iranian Sufi poet, Hafiz, wrote:

"How

Fascinating the idea of death

Can be.

Too bad, though,

Because

It just isn't

True."[27]

FOOTNOTES

1. Morton Kelsey, *Afterlife: The Other Side of Dying,* Paulist Press, New York, 1979, page 108.
2. Cited by Alan Gauld, *Mediumship and Survival,* Heinemann, London, 1982, pages 42-43.
3. Hornell Hart, *The Enigma of Survival,* Rider and Company, London, 1959, pages 74-75.
4. Cited by Robert Almeder, *Death and Personal Survival,* Littlefield Adams, Lanham, Md., 1992, pages 205-206.
5. Cited by Alan Gauld, *Op. Cit.,* pages 47-48.
6. Gary Schwartz, *The Afterlife Experiments: Breakthrough Scientific Evidence of Life After Death,* Pocket Books, New York, 2002, page XVI.
7. *Ibid.,* pages 235-236.
8. "The Accuracy and Replicability of Anomalous After-Death Communication Across Highly Skilled Mediums," by Schwartz, Russek, Nelson and Barentsen , *Journal of*

the Society for Psychical Research, Vol. 65.1, No. 862, pages 1-25. Also see website http://www.openmindsciences.com/hbo-exp.htm

9. For a critical study of the case involving five mediums, see "Accuracy and Replicability of Anomalous After-Death Communication Across Highly Skilled Mediums: A Critique," by Richard Wiseman and Ciaran O'Keeffe, Richard Wiseman and Ciaran O'Keeffe, *Paranormal Review,* Issue 19, 2001, pages 3-6.

10. Bill and Judy Guggenheim, *Hello From Heaven,* Bantam Books, New York, 1995, pages 25-26.

11. *Ibid.,* page 46.

12. Cited by Louis LaGrand, *After Death Communication: Final Farewells,* Llewellyn Publications, St. Paul, 1998, pages 44-45.

13. Cited by Kelsey, *Op. Cit.,* page 95.

14. Guggenheim, *Op. Cit.,* page 66.

15. Celia Green and Charles McCreery, *Apparitions,* Hamish Hamilton, Ltd., London, 1975, page 52.

16. Guggenheim, *Op, Cit., page 122.*

17. *Ibid.,* pages 133-134.

18. From "Paranormal Contacts With the Dying: 14 Contemporary Death Coincidences," by Sylvia H. Wright in *Journal of the Society for Psychical Research,* Vol. 63, Number 57, October 1999, page 263.

19. From "Spontaneous Psychokinesis After Bereavement," by Sylvia H. Wright, in *Journal of the Society for Psychical Research,* Vol. 62, Number 52, July 1998, page 389.

20. Green and McCreery, *Op. Cit.,* page 163.

21. LaGrand, *Op. Cit.,* pages 92-93.

22. Guggenheim, *Op. Cit.,* page 282.

23. G. Scott Sparrow, *I Am With You Always,* Bantam Books, New York, 1995, pages 78-79.

24. The Guggenheims offer a longer discussion of these suggestions, which are summarized here. *Op. Cit.,* pages 375-382.

25. For an expanded and passionate discussion of these points, see "Who's Afraid of Life After Death?" by Neal Grossman, in *Journal of Near Death* Studies, Vol. 21, Number 1, Fall 2002, pages 21-24.

26. Stanislav Groff, *Beyond the Brain,* New York: State University of New York Press, 1985.

27. Daniel Ladinsky, translator, *The Gift: Poems by Hafiz,* Penguin Putnam Inc., New York, 1999, page 301.

INDEX

BIBLIOGRAPHY

Almeder, Robert. *Death and Personal Survival.* Lanham, MD: Rowman Littlefield, 1992.

Atwater, P. M. H. *Beyond the Light.* New York: Birch Lane Press, 1995.

Bayless, Raymond and McAdams, Elizabeth. *The Case for Life After Death: Parapsychologists Look at Survival Evidence.* Chicago: Nelson Hall, 1981.

Becker, Carl. *Paranormal Experience and Survival of Death.* Albany: State University of New York, 1993.

Blackmore, Susan. *Beyond the Body.* Chicago: Academy Publishers, 1982.

Bowman, Carol and Steve. *Children's Past Lives: How Past Life Memories Affect Your Child.* New York: Bantam, 1998.

Crookall, Robert. *The Supreme Adventure.* London: James Clark, 1961.

Crookall, Robert. *Casebook of Astral Projection.* Seacacus, NJ: Citadel Press, 1980.

Currie, Ian. *You Cannot Die.* Toronto: Somerville House, 1998.

Gauld, Alan. *Mediumship and Survival.* London: Heinemann, 1982.

Greenhouse, Herbert. *The Astral Journey.* New York: Avon Books, 1974.

Hart, Hornell. *The Enigma of Survival.* Springfield, IL: Thomas, 1952.

Hick, John. *Death and Eternal Life.* San Francisco: Harper and Row, 1976.

Jacobson, Nils. *Life Without Death.* New York: Dell, 1974.

Moody, Raymond. *Life After Life.* New York: Bantam Books, 1977.

Moody, Raymond. *The Light Beyond.* New York: Bantam Books, 1998.

Morse, Melvin. *Closer to the Light.* New York: Ivy Books, 1990.

Myers, F.W.H. *Human Personality and its Survival of Bodily Death.* Charlottesville, Va: Hampton Roads Publishing, 2001.

Osis, Karlis and Haraldsson, Erlendur. *At the Hour of Death.* New York: Avon, 1977.

Ring, Kenneth. *Lessons From the Light.* Portsmouth, NH: Moment Point Press, 1998.

Stevenson, Ian. *Twenty Cases Suggestive of Reincarnation.* Charlottesville, VA: University Press of Virginia, 1974.

Stevenson, Ian. *Where Reincarnation and Biology Intersect.* Westport, CT: Praeger, 1997.

Tart, Charles. *Mind Body Spirit.* Charlottesville, VA: Hampton Roads Publishing Company, 1997.

Woolger, Roger. *Other Lives, Other Selves.* New York: Bantam New Age Books, 1998.

INTERNET KEY WORDS:

NEAR DEATH EXPERIENCE

NEAR DEATH EXPERIENCE RESEARCH

DEATHBED VISIONS

SURVIVAL OF BODILY DEATH

OUT-OF-BODY EXPERIENCE RESEARCH FOUNDATION

PARAPSYCHOLOGY AND PERSONAL SURVIVAL AFTER DEATH

REINCARNATION RESEARCH

IAN STEVENSON

APPARITIONS AND SURVIVAL OF DEATH

AFTER DEATH COMMUNICATIONS

BEREAVEMENT SUPPORT GROUP

IANDS (International Association for Near-Death Studies)